KERRY
THE AUTOBIOGRAPHY

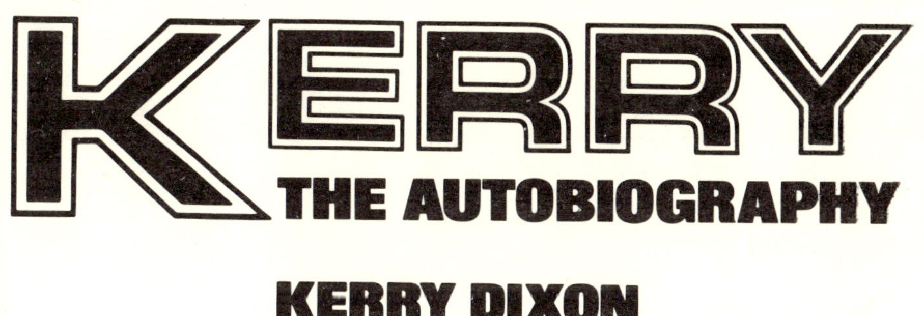

KERRY DIXON

Macdonald
Queen Anne Press

A Queen Anne Press BOOK

First published in Great Britain in 1986 by
Queen Anne Press, a division of
Macdonald & Co (Publishers) Ltd
Greater London House, Hampstead Road,
London NW1 7QX

A BPCC plc Company

British Library Cataloguing in Publication Data

Dixon, Kerry
Kerry Dixon autobiography.
1. Dixon, Kerry 2. Soccer players———
England———Biography
I. Title
796.334'092'4 GV942.7.D5/

ISBN 0-356-12355-3

Typeset by Cylinder Typesetting Ltd, London

Reproduced, printed and bound in Great Britain by
Hazell Watson & Viney Limited,
Member of the BPCC Group,
Aylesbury, Bucks

Special thanks to Mum, Dad and sister Jane, and to all relatives and friends who have helped me to get where I am today, and without whose help I believe I certainly would not have achieved what I have.

Special wishes go to Ron Fullbrook, Brendan McNally, Maurice Evans, John Neal, Brian Roach and the current Chelsea staff whose support and belief in my ability has enabled me to reach a level which many a time I thought impossible to reach.

Finally, thanks go to Les Harriott, Mike Justin, Dennis Diggin, John Dolan, Michelle, Gemma and Kelly for being such good friends.

CONTENTS

1

DON'T CRY FOR ME MARADONA

There is no other place on earth I would rather have been at high noon on 22nd June, 1986 than inside the spectacular Estadio Azteca of Mexico City. England versus Argentina, in the quarter-finals of the World Cup, was a momentous occasion in its own right. The fact this was to be the first major sporting link between the two countries since the Falklands War four years previously ensured the eyes of the world were focused on the twenty-two players who walked side by side out into the arena. Leading the Argentinians was a small, dark, swarthy figure with a barrel chest and enormous thighs. How we would come to know and respect him. He was Diego Armando Maradona. Within an hour he had all but destroyed England and caused me to believe he was the greatest player I had ever seen. I had been bitterly disappointed when the England manager, Bobby Robson, had named his team to face Argentina. I was not included even among the five substitutes. No one, either at home or in Mexico, had expected the manager to change his team following a spectacular revival after a poor start to the competition. But I confess I had hoped to be named as one of the players on the substitutes bench to be called upon in emergency. And yet I remained full of hope and optimism because I genuinely believed England would beat Argentina that day and I might yet be able to play a decisive part in the World Cup.

I cherished memories of the Azteca Stadium from the previous year when I had been a member of the England party which had travelled to Mexico for a summer tournament. It was in that stadium, on my first full appearance for my country, that I scored two goals in a terrific 3–0 triumph over West Germany. But the place was different now. When I had played there the stadium was barely half full. This time the atmosphere was electric with an official attendance recorded at a staggering 114,580. The national flags of all the competing countries in the 1986 World Cup finals were flying; the noise from horns and drums was deafening; masses of gaily coloured bunting created a carnival mood; and yet beneath it all there was a hushed expectancy about the place. Previously, I had believed the Azteca Stadium was possibly the finest theatre for football in the world. On that day I was convinced of it. I would have given anything to have been out there playing against the Argentinians. Instead I was confined to an Independent Television commentary box situated behind one of the goals. With me were Mark Hateley, previously my great rival for the centre forward position, along with Gary Bailey, Viv Anderson and Alvin Martin.

The opening half was tight and tense with our strikers Gary Lineker and Peter Beardsley marked closely by Jose Luis Cuciuffo and Oscar Alfredo Ruggeri, with Jose Luis Brown in a sweeper role. For one wonderful moment we thought Beardsley had put us in front after a slip by the Argentine goalkeeper Nery Pumpido. From a very acute angle Peter managed to get in a shot but the ball flew into the side netting. In the event, neither team had managed to execute a breakthrough before half-time and, although Argentina appeared to have enjoyed the better of the exchanges, I knew the England boys would be reasonably satisfied with their work in those opening forty-five minutes of the match. The Argentinians had made no secret of their intent to snatch an early goal and then snuff out any England attempt at a reprisal. In fact, our excellent goalkeeper, Peter Shilton, had not been threatened seriously until five minutes into the second half when all hell broke loose in an incident which was to prove the most controversial of the entire World Cup.

Steve Hodge, who had proved to be a revelation in the almost impossible role of replacing our injured captain Bryan Robson, attempted to relieve the pressure on the edge of our penalty area by playing the ball back to Shilton. As the goalkeeper came to collect, Maradona darted forward and suddenly the ball was in the net. From my position at the far side of the ground I had not detected illegal contact by the Argentina captain, but Mark Hateley was certain that Maradona had punched the ball with his arm to beat Shilton's challenge. We dashed over to the television monitor where the slow-motion play-back revealed conclusively that Maradona had, indeed, handled the ball. Unfortunately, neither the Tunisian referee nor his Bulgarian and Costa Rican linesmen were privy to the astonishing and conclusive evidence being placed before the world by television at that moment. It would be unfair to accuse the officials of being the only people in the entire stadium not to see the handling offence. Maradona had certainly fooled me as well.

The England players, especially Shilton, protested at the injustice of the goal but we all knew in out heart of hearts that the goal would be allowed to stand. Rarely do officials change their minds in such a situation and this was a clear case of the referee simply failing to observe the offence in question. Many of us had believed at the outset of the match that one goal, either way, might determine the outcome. Perhaps the controversy would have raged longer and fiercer had Maradona not provided a further outrageous example of his influence on the fortunes of Argentina and England. This time the contribution was born from sheer, incredible genius.

Five minutes had elapsed since his handled goal and England were slowly recovering their composure when Maradona picked up the ball in the centre circle. Almost like a world champion skier on the giant slalom he set off on a run which took him beyond the challenges of defender after defender. I'll swear the ball was tied to his bootlaces as he sped into the England penalty area, side-stepped Shilton and scored, just as Terry Butcher was attempting another last-ditch intervention. The silence was almost deafening in the ITV commentary box. The players out on the pitch couldn't believe it either. The looks of incredulity on their faces said it all. My own emotions were a crazy mixture of sadness for England and my mates out there on the field and an irrepressible feeling of privilege that I had been there to witness the greatest goal I have ever seen.

The England lads responded magnificently. Tottenham winger Chris Waddle was sent on and shortly afterwards he was joined by the Watford left winger John Barnes. The idea was to spread the Argentine defence as wide as possible by attacking them down the flanks. The strategy almost worked because in the end England failed by a whisker to save the match. I was particularly pleased that Barnes had finally been given an opportunity to demonstrate his fabulous skills in the World Cup. I had shared a room with him during the seven weeks we had spent preparing for the World Cup and, more than anyone else, knew of the frustration he had experienced at being on the sidelines. This was his golden opportunity and he took it in style. With just ten minutes of the match remaining he beat his man out on the left wing and crossed the ball perfectly for Gary Lineker to pull a goal back. Argentina were wilting, clearly afraid of the goalscoring reputation of Lineker – a sight which warmed my heart particularly.

An identical move, with John Barnes again providing a fabulous centre, almost brought the equaliser with just three minutes remaining. Gary moved to head in the cross and it looked a goal all the way but suddenly he was flat on his back and the ball had been cleared. Gary told me later that he, too, had been convinced he was about to score when a terrific bang on the nape of his neck sent him sprawling and knocked him out; a tragedy for England because if an equaliser had been forthcoming at that moment I'm convinced we would have gone on to win the match and, who knows, possibly the World Cup. However, John Barnes had done his job and I could not have been more delighted for him. He is a super player and a super bloke and the kind of crosses he provided against Argentina were a striker's dream. But like me, he had been captivated by the sheer genius of Maradona.

I refuse to condemn the little Argentinian for the handled goal. I don't think I would have attempted to punch the ball in a similar situation and would have gone for it with my head. Nevertheless, he did it, got away with it and went on to lift the World Cup. Let's be fair about it, if Lineker or Beardsley had done the same thing for England we would not have been complaining too loudly. What Maradona did was a form of cheating but there is a old saying in football which goes 'there is no such thing as a bad goal'. As a dedicated goalscorer myself I have to admit I follow that creed. The theory that had Maradona not got away with his first goal he would have been unable to have scored his magnificent second effort has subsequently been advanced. Certainly, the fact that England were suddenly chasing the match in a sudden-death situation meant the players had to push forward and so leave greater gaps in the midfield and defence. But in my book it would be churlish to attempt to deride one of the greatest goals the World Cup competition has ever seen. Only a very rare and special player could have contemplated scoring it. The theory loses its credibility, in any event, when a further sensational goal from Maradona in the semi-final against Belgium is considered. The little man is the greatest player of his generation and proved in the 1986 World Cup that he possesses the talent, skill, initiative and confidence to execute goals like that at any given moment.

The mood in the England dressing room after that quarter-final was understandably sombre. The entire squad of twenty-two players who had worked so hard and so long to bring success to our country were deeply depressed. We'd come back from an uncertain start in the qualifying groups to rekindle our hopes and ambitions of a World Cup triumph. But the dressing room after the game was not the place for sensible analysis and none was attempted. We returned to our hotel situated next to the Mexico City airport where the manager called us together for one last team meeting. He thanked us all and told us that we had been a great squad of players both on and off the field – a credit to our country. We had worked terrifically hard. We had done our best.

There was nothing left for us to do but return home. The

World Cup was over as far as England was concerned. I watched the final on television down in Torquay where I had gone to spend a few days holiday. The fact that West Germany had reached the final had not surprised me as I had become more and more impressed by their play and organisation as the tournament progressed. Compared with the devastation that Maradona had caused in the quarter-finals against England and the semi-finals with Belgium, it could be said that Diego Maradona had a quiet game. The fact is he had a hand in all of Argentina's three goals which provided a 3–2 victory.

Hundred of players from all around the world had prepared diligently during the previous four years not only to reach the Mexican finals but also to take part in them. At the end of the day, on 29th June 1986, the World Cup had been narrowed down to one remarkable little man. It had become the Diego Armando Maradona Cup.

WORLD CUP IN WAITING

I was full of hope, ambition and expectancy when I joined up with the other twenty-one players selected to represent England in the World Cup Finals at a Heathrow Airport hotel on 6th May, 1986. It had been a good day all round. Earlier I had signed a new sponsorship deal with the Town and Country Car Rental Company, which included an agreement that I would be supplied with a Ford Granada 2.8cc Ghia car. But the major excitement was generated by the fact I had at last begun to believe that I was actually going to Mexico.

Umbro, the sports goods manufacturers who were providing England's equipment, issued all of the players with suits, leisure wear and a hold-all and after a painful jab in the backside to innoculate us against the threat of hepatitis in Mexico we were off to a Government reception. We returned to the hotel at 8.00pm, enjoyed a comfortable dinner and were off to bed by 11.00pm.

I was to share a room with Watford's John Barnes for the duration of the trip, which suited me because the two of us had become firm friends and frequently met up socially. But sleep was not easy to come by that night. My adrenalin was flowing and I found it impossible to curb my excitement and anticipation of what might be in store over the next couple of weeks. I was still having to pinch myself to believe I had actually made it into England's World Cup squad. Memories flooded back: the hours of painstaking practice with Dad; the clips around the ears from Mum when she had believed I wasn't taking my responsibilities seriously enough; the pain and humiliation of rejection by my home team Luton; being turned away from Tottenham when it seemed my ability to score goals was not enough to ensure a career as a professional footballer; the happy days with non-league Dunstable; the fight-back at Reading; the goals which made me a success at Chelsea and as an international player.

Kerry Dixon was going to Mexico with England and the realisation that but for Mike and Anne Dixon I would still have been stuck in an engineering factory in Luton rushing home from work to catch the World Cup matches on television filled me with gratitude. Many is the time a starry-eyed young lad has approached me and asked: 'How do I get to become a top footballer, Kerry?' My answer is always the same. 'A bit of talent and a Mum and Dad like mine and you won't go far wrong.' I have been lucky enough to enjoy and prosper from the support, love and devotion of a closely-knit family. I have always been conscious that my Mum, Dad, sister Jane, grandparents, aunties, uncles and mates I have known and cherished since schooldays have been behind me every step of the way. The only way I have been able to repay that faith and encouragement has been in the small success I have achieved as a professional footballer.

I was not yet twenty-five and perhaps my best and most successful years as a professional footballer lie ahead. I was aware that, all things being equal, I could expect to reach the peak of my powers in time for the 1990 World Cup Finals due to be held in Italy. But I was absolutely determined to make the most of the moment and to seize my opportunity if it was to be presented to me. Although Mark Hateley was considered first choice ahead of me for the number nine shirt I was determined to exert as much pressure as possible on him. Every single player in that squad harboured his own private hopes and ambitions for the Mexico World Cup and none of us intended going along for the ride. That fact soon become apparent in the days and weeks leading up to the opening game.

I was awake at 8.30am the following morning and, after an embarrassing episode when my hold-all developed a split in its side, we were off to Gatwick for the flight to America. The press photographers were out in force and television cameras followed our every move. It all added to the occasion. The flight was long and tiring. We were eight hours in the air, two hours at St Louis airport before transferring to another aircraft for a further two hours journey into Colorado Springs. Colorado had been chosen as an ideal situation for the two weeks acclimatisation programme to the kind of heat and altitude we would have to combat in Mexico. The joke was on us the next morning when we reported for training – it was snowing!

There are not enough superlatives to describe adequately the sheer magnificence of the Broadmoor Hotel in Colorado Springs that was to be our headquarters for the next couple of weeks. The views were breathtaking with a lake situated in front of the hotel beneath a spectacular back-drop provided by the Rockie Mountains. Four gourmet restaurants, a well situated swimming pool area plus two championship golf courses completed the scene. All of our training was to be conducted at the United States Air Force Academy up in the hills, about one hour's drive by coach from the hotel. This, too, was quite magnificent. The setting was peaceful and restful with swimming pool and sauna facilities which would help to build up the resistance of the body to high temperatures. I wanted to savour and remember every moment and, to this end, began to keep a diary which I compiled each evening. I noted on Friday, 9th May that the weather had begun to improve. Just as well, because on that day we walked almost three miles up the mountain to test out the altitude. The scenery was incredible, and a few of the players, including Mark Hateley, Glenn Hoddle, Kenny Sansom and I decided to run down the mountain dodging around the rocks. It was a great run, very exhilarating and destined to be repeated on several occasions. Then it was straight into the steam-room to build up the temperature resistance once more.

Perhaps the diary I kept will provide the most accurate illustration of England's preparations for the World Cup and reveal my innermost feelings about events as and when they occurred.

Saturday, 10th May

Awoke at 7.30am. It's 2.30pm at home so decide to telephone before FA Cup Final gets underway. Shocked to hear the news that David Speedie, my striking partner at Chelsea, has been left out of the Scotland World Cup squad. I understood he had been promised a place by the Scotland manager Alex Ferguson. Felt terribly sorry for him. It had been bad enough for me sweating about whether I would be selected let alone being left out after being promised a place. England players decide to hold a 'sweep' on first goalscorer in the FA Cup Final between Everton and Liverpool. I draw Ian Rush. I'm well pleased about that. News filters through that Gary Lineker has scored for Everton (I'll throttle him when he arrives here on Monday). Liverpool win 3–1 and Rush scores two goals. Just my luck!

Regular weigh-in session at 12.45. I've put on four pounds. I can't believe it! I've eaten hardly anything. Some of the other lads were up by six pounds. Training lasts for ninety minutes. The ball travels further through the thin air – will have to get used to that. Called in at a hamburger joint on the way back to hotel. Sandwiches with chips arrived. I didn't eat any. I want the four pounds off as quickly as possible. Most of the other players have the same idea – they don't eat anything either. Back at hotel watch a video film of the FA Cup Final. Not a bad game. It's my ambition to play in that match one day.

Sunday, 11th May

Best night's sleep yet. Breakfast in the hotel golf club. Views really are spectacular. Lounge around swimming pool for a while. Tea and toast at midday. First game in the afternoon against the US Air Force. They can't be too bad because Canada only beat them 1–0. Weight check: 13st 8lb – one pound over. Manager announces team. Mark Hateley, as expected, in number nine shirt. I am on the substitute bench. I'm determined to make a fight of it in that position. I wonder if the manager has made up his mind finally as to who will be first choice. Ah well, I'll soon find out. I'm told I will play for a least one half of the match. Mark hits a hat-trick as England 4–0 up at the interval. I start the second half. John Barnes, my roommate, also anxious to impress. He wants to get in team as well. John makes my first goal. I end up with three, the last goal making it 11–0 for England. I've equalled Mark's performance. Coach Don Howe remarked that my turning of defenders had improved dramatically and asked if I had been working on it. I told him I had.

Monday, 12th May

Day off. Tried to play tennis with John Barnes and Viv Anderson but have to abandon the idea because a kick on the calf in yesterday's game has stiffened up. Telephone home in afternoon to discover to my absolute delight that the kids' football team I coach has pulled off a league and cup double. The news puts me in a great mood. The Everton players, along with some of the press, arrive at hotel. Where is that Lineker?

Tuesday, 13th May

Medical checks. Blood and urine samples to test players' reaction to altitude. Training. Fast burst of 660 yards followed by immediate pulse readings. Pulses read every six minutes to check on recovery rates. Into steam room. Manager comments about my turning of defenders. Couple of games of chess with John Barnes. Lights out 11.15pm.

Wednesday, 14th May

Another game today. This one against South Korea who have also qualified to play in World Cup Finals. Not in team again but promised opportunity in second half. Mark scores first and Bryan Robson gets another in 2–0 half-time lead. Korea not bad at all. Determined to do well and get a couple of goals. Just miss with a header early on but on target from another great cross from Barnesy. Ray Wilkins hit a nice through ball, used pace to carry me through and poke a second goal for myself. Beat Korea 4–1 in the end and am pleased with my overall game. Good day all round when I beat Barnesy 3–2 in a chess match.

Thursday, 15th May

Awoken by telephone call from my girlfriend, Michelle. Along with other players' wives and girlfriends she is coming out to Colorado next week. Players ordered to meet at the pool for a series of swimming exercises to loosen muscles before real training session. Photographers everywhere. They had a field day. More than I can say for myself. Training in afternoon a nightmare. Nothing would go right for me in shooting practice. Not a day to remember.

Friday, 16th May

Leaving for Los Angeles for a game against the World Cup hosts Mexico on Saturday. Important game for me this. Determined to get on pitch to put more pressure on Mark. Rumour goes around that I'll be on from the start. I'll believe it when it happens! Takes six hours to get to LA. I'm whacked. Bed by 10.00pm.

Saturday, 17th May

Tea and toast at 12.00pm. Just as I thought – Mark is playing. I am one of substitutes. No more than I expected really. Manager's team talk stresses the great interest at home and urges the need for an impressive performance. Los Angeles Coliseum brings back memories of two goals I scored last summer against United States team. It's hot. Mark gets two great goals. Peter Beardsley scores another and I get a chance with about seventeen minutes left. I replace Mark but I know in my heart of hearts he has already booked his place in the team in the World Cup opener against Portugal with those two super goals. Still, I thought I did quite well in brief time against Mexico. Had a good shot on the turn which was inches over the bar. Straight to airport for return to Colorado. Arrive at midnight. Wives and girlfriends have arrived.

Sunday, 18th May
Day off from football. Time to enjoy the hotel. Take a stroll round the lake. Beautiful. Mr Robson and Mr Wragg (Chairman of International Committee) welcome wives and girlfriends at a nice lunch.

Monday, 19th May
Weather has been hot for a while now but getting used to the sun. Training in afternoon. Manager believes we slackened off too much in second half against Mexico. Train for forty-five minutes, rest for ten minutes, train for another forty-five minutes. Just like a match. The heat in Monterrey is getting closer. Stay longer in the steam room to prepare for it. Allowed out of the hotel for a restaurant meal. If you're ever in Colorado try Finn's Fish restaurant. Had a lovely meal and pleasant night with Barnesy and girlfriend. Another late night — in bed by 10.00pm.

Tuesday, 20th May
Michelle has stomach trouble. Maybe it's altitude sickness or too much sun. Shows the dangers. Further evidence after breakfast when the girlfriend of Tottenham's Gary Stevens fainted. Not serious, thankfully. Dr Edwards soon has her up and about. The hottest day so far. Within half an hour it's cloudy and dull. Heavy rain expected. It's amazing how weather changes here in so short a time. Training in afternoon for forty-five minutes and then the dreaded 660 yard burst. ITV's Jim Rosenthal has a go at it. Runs well but looks as though he's found it difficult. Formal dress for dinner in evening. Bed at 11.00pm.

Wednesday, 21st May
Training once again for the full one and half hours. Steam room turned up to maximum temperature. Boy, it's hot. Cinema in evening. Film is 'Back to Future'. I wonder what it holds for me in this World Cup!

Thursday, 22nd May
Photographs taken which will be presented to all of the players as mementos of membership of England squad of 1986. Full training session as usual. A touch of drama when we are unable to return to dressing rooms at US Academy because of mercury spillage. Mr Robson took the opportunity to hold an impromptu team meeting and as we sprawled out on the grass informed us of the team to play against Canada on Saturday. Substitute again – I couldn't expect any better after Mark's performance against Mexico. Allowed to pick up our clothes after half an hour. Splendid last night with wives and girlfriends back at hotel with a super dinner laid on by Football Association.

Friday, 23rd May
Left for Vancouver at 11.30am. Girls leaving hotel at 2.00pm. Another tiring day travelling with a coach trip to Denver and half hour wait in Seattle. Bed at 10.00pm.

Saturday, 24th May
Game starts at 11.00am. Up at 7.30am. Unusual preparation for a football match! About 7,000 people at game. Not a good match at all. England didn't play too well. The major story as far as the newspapers was concerned was injury to Gary Lineker. He was rushed off to hospital with a suspected broken wrist after taking a heavy tumble. Thankfully, the injury is only a sprain. He's replaced on the pitch by Peter Beardsley. What a reception he received. He was once a popular player here with Vancouver Whitecaps. Disappointment for me because I didn't get on to the pitch. Still determined to keep the pressure on Mark even though I believe he has slowly ensured he will be the number one centre forward when Mexico begins. He played quite well and scored another goal in the 1–0 win over Canada.

Sunday, 25th May
Out of bed at 5.00am. Mexico at last. What a tiring day. Flight to Los Angeles with a five hour wait at LA airport for flight to

Monterrey. Just about to leave when another passenger begins to rant and rave that his luggage had not been loaded on the aircraft. We look out of the window and see all of our bags on the tarmac. Crew explain that because of weight luggage will be sent on later. Not a good flight. Loads of ups and downs and lots of turbulence. Half of an hour out from Monterrey captain calmly informs passengers that fuel has run low and he will be have to land. Bit of panic among the lads. Goalkeeper Chris Woods, a nervous passenger at the best of times, was as white as sheet. The plane seemed to be going in very quickly. Glenn Hoddle shouted that he couldn't see the runway. That caused more panic. What a relief when we finally threaded a way through an electrical storm and landed safely. None of us was looking forward to getting back into the air again but the final leg of the journey into Monterrey was uneventful. Mind you, it took double the scheduled time because of severe head-winds. Pandemonium at Monterrey airport. Press and television everywhere. Finally left for sixty-mile drive to our World Cup headquarters in Saltillo up in the hills. Amazing scenes. Police escort of seven cars with all the occupants armed to the teeth. Even armed guards situated on the team coach itself. After eighteen hours of travelling just grateful to drop into bed at 11.00pm. Boy am I tired!

Monday, 26th May

Awake at 9.00am but still feel very tired. Relaxed by swimming pool. Immediately aware that the heat and humidity were much different to Colorado – the sweat pouring out of me. Training will be an ordeal. Left for training ground in Monterrey at 1.15pm. Another incredible journey. Police car leads team coach with two unmarked security vehicles alongside and another police car behind. Travel at a terrific pace with every road, every side-track adjoining the main highway sealed off by police. It's exciting but will take a lot of getting used to if this is to be the normal situation throughout our stay. Scenery spectacular. Road cuts down to Monterrey between rocky, unforgiving mountain range that shimmers in the heat. Arrive at training headquarters which is called the Cima Club at 2.30pm. Again security is tight, armed guards on gates. Not even massive contingent of press and television can outnumber them. Training begins. In no time at all I'm exhausted. I'm not the only one either. Looking around everybody is struggling. It's a nightmare. We'd expected it to be tough in the heat but not as bad as this! Training scheduled to last for a full ninety minutes with a ten minute break in between. At last it's half-time. Dr Vernon Edwards takes pulse readings. We are all impressed by the thoroughness of the preparation for this competition. Body temperature caused the most concern. Mine up only slightly but Chris Waddle hits 104 degrees. The doctor is unperturbed. He expected wild variations, it seems. Every player was weighed before and after training. Incredibly, I had lost five pounds during the session. At 12st 13lb that was the lightest I had been in four years. Reaction set in on the return journey to Saltillo Hotel. Felt sick, giddy and light-headed. Feared I would not make it without vomiting. Doctor diagnoses heat-exhaustion and tells me to drink plenty of fluids. Three bottles of purified water and two cans of orange later felt better. Managed a bit of dinner and more water before flopping out at 10.00pm. I think this day made all the players realise that without acclimatisation we would have been in desperate trouble. I hope I feel better tomorrow.

Tuesday, 27th May

Wake at 10.00am. That's late for me. Feel slightly better but not one hundred per cent. Team meeting at 11.00am. Manager imposes sunbathing curfew after 11.15am, which is sensible in these conditions. I'm told to stay out of sun altogether by doctor. All players spend a lot of time watching television sports channel ESPN. French Open tennis currently being shown. Characters within the squad beginning to emerge. Peter Beardsley becoming known as the organiser. Aston Villa's Steve Hodge definitely the most forgetful. Lost his sweater and a key to his locker and always forgets what to wear on special occasions. I've been nicknamed 'Ernie'. It seems my hairstyle is shared by Ernie Wise! Peter Shilton now known as 'Shilly' after Mr Robson had inadvertently used the name in a training session. It all adds to the camaraderie among the players which is absolutely first class. Leave for training at 1.15pm. Here we go again down the mountain. Much better this time. Plenty of water to drink before, during and after. Even so, some of the lads found to have high body temperature after session. All had a swim in the club pool before returning to base. Special games room set up in hotel. I play pool while other players go off to video room to watch one of the many films we have brought out to Mexico. Games room well equipped with plenty of games and books to keep us occupied. Boredom not a problem, thank goodness.

Wednesday, 28th May

Sleepless night – don't know why. Phone call from England at 8.20am. Nice to keep up with the news from home. Another match day. We are due to play Monterrey who have just won the Mexican club championship. We hear it is going to be televised in England. Manager says he intends to give a full game to the players in the squad who have not had much match practice so far. Good news for me then. Spent hour by the swimming pool then telephoned Mun and Dad who wished me all the best in the game. I know they will be rooting for me. Dad gives the usual advice to play it simple and if the chance of a goal comes along to go for it. The strategy has worked well for me over the last few years. Tea and toast at 1.15pm and leave for Monterrey a quarter of an hour later. Monterrey proved good opposition. I scored England's first two goals and made the third for my mate Barnesy. Gary Stevens got the last goal in a 4–1 win. England still seem to be big news. Reporters and photographers out in force. Few interviews after the game and plenty of autograph signing. Weigh-in shows I've lost five pounds during the game. Manager calls the players together. It looks serious. It is. Dr Edwards, who has become a great pal of the lads, had been taken ill during the match. We are told he suffered a heart-attack and has been rushed into intensive care department of the Monterrey hospital. Full details about his condition are not known. We are all stunned. The happy mood after another encouraging England performance has been killed. The Doc's illness seems to have put everything into perspective. We have all worked hard to try and do well for ourselves and our country. The doc had dedicated himself to our cause but now he was fighting for his life. Hardly a sound on the team bus returning to Saltillo. Dinner at 8.15pm. Mr Robson confirms that the Doc has suffered a massive heart-attack. His wife, back in England, must be informed. What an awful job.

Thursday, 29th May

Awake at 9.30am. Much better news about the Doc. He has had a comfortable night and the signs are good. Everybody cheers up. Unusual training session – it's raining. Quiet day all round.

Friday, 30th May

Awake at 9.30am. Don't feel too well. Identification badges issued to all of the players for the World Cup. Security will be tight. Training plans changed. Pitch in Monterrey water-logged! New ground found in Saltillo. Left hotel at 2.15pm. Pitch very sticky and mud everywhere. I had headache and sore throat. Conditioned worsened as time went on. Decided to see doctor. ITV's physician standing in for Dr Edwards while Arsenal's Dr John Crane arrives from England to take over. Television doctor a very feminine lady. Prescribed tablets to take away headache and instructed to inhale over steaming water to clear my sinuses. Told to stay in my room. Rest of squad attend official function in Monterrey. I'm happy enough to stick with a sleeping tablet and bed at 10.00pm.

Saturday, 31st May

Wake at 8.15am. Doc visits at 8.30am. I was on telephone to home. Arrange to see her later. Felt much better but she insists on more capsules while inhaling steam. World Cup begins today – I'd almost forgotten! Italy, the holders, play Bulgaria. It's live on television at midday. All players watch match. Opinion is Italy unlucky not to win. Miss many chances and Bulgaria equalise in last five minutes for a 1–1 draw. Training again in Saltillo, this time at Portugal's headquarters who we meet in the opening game on Tuesday. After work-out we play a team of Mexican twelve-year-olds. Good public relations exercise and the players enjoy it. Result: 5–5 draw. One goal for me and plenty of new friends. ITV tell us they will provide recordings of World Cup matches we will miss because of our own training schedule. They entertain us to drinks and we make a presentation to their doctor for the invaluable work she has done for the players. Watch special video put together by ITV. Bed at 10.00pm.

Sunday, 1st June

Wake at 9.30am. Team meeting at 11.00am. The manager names his team to meet Portugal tomorrow. It was the team everyone expected – I am not in it. Watched Brazil versus Spain on television – poor game in my opinion. Controversy because Spain scored a good goal not allowed by referee. My view that England can do very well in the World Cup is not affected by this match. Training in Monterrey at Technologico Stadium where we will play our first two matches. Nice place with flower beds and privet hedging in front of dressing rooms. Practice match for an hour. Talked in morning about set-piece attacks like throw-ins and free kicks. Now put theory into practice. Dinner at 8.00pm. Played pool and watched television for short while. Bed at midnight – late for me.

Monday, 2nd June

Wake at 9.30am. Training in Saltillo. Light session. Run through of set-pieces again. The manager names his substitutes. Terribly disappointed because I am not among them, although half expected it because of the cover that would be needed on the bench. Begin to wonder if Mr Robson will ever change the substitutes. Depressed. Watched football on television in afternoon and played pool in evening.

Tuesday, 3rd June

Wake at 10.00am. Big day for England – first World Cup game against Portugal. Tea and toast at midday. Watch Mexico v Belgium game. Still believe England will do well. Arrive at Technologico Stadium at 2.30pm. Loads of English fans at stadium. Substitutes and remainder of squad went out first followed by two teams. Portugal definitely playing for a draw with a five man midfield. Instead they pull off a shock win scoring through Carlos Manuel on the one occasion England's defensive work a bit slack. Everybody disappointed in dressing room afterwards. Manager insists: 'It's not over yet, lift up your heads.' Arrived back at Saltillo hotel and played tennis with Barnesy, Viv Anderson and Alvin Martin. Good facilities at hotel. Even tennis courts are floodlit. Still playing at 11.00pm.

Wednesday, 4th June

Derby day in England. ITV arrange for players to see the race. Arsenal's Kenny Sansom and Tottenham's Glenn Hoddle are the bookies. They take players bets on the World Cup matches and agree to provide similar service on Derby. I back Dancing Brave. Finishes an unlucky second. Breakfast at 9.00am. It's the hottest day so far in Mexico. What a scorcher. Midday visit to BBC hotel nearby and watch West Germany against Uruguay. Impressed by the Germans. I think they can go a long way. Get well deserved draw against Uruguay with equaliser five minutes from end. Uruguayans diving all over the place after tackles. This kind of acting is becoming a major factor in the competition. Training in Saltillo for the players who had not been used against Portugal. Good session. Returned to hotel just in time to see Scotland lose 1–0 to Denmark. Team meeting at 6.00pm. Mr Robson gave his views and some players ironed out a few discrepancies in a constructive, general discussion.

Thursday, 5th June

Early start. Sunbathing by swimming pool but under orders to cover up after 11.00am. Watched France against USSR on television. Two good teams. Finished at 1–1. Training back in Monterrey. Manager named same team to play against Morocco in second match. Substitutes to be announced on day of game. Had glass of orange juice with Dave Faulder, pal from Luton, over in Mexico for the World Cup. Bed at 11.00pm.

Friday, 6th June

Wake 9.30am. Sunbathing banned on day of match. Team meeting at 11.00am. Manager names same substitutes as game against Portugal. Disappointed again. I'd hoped Mr Robson would have me on bench to go on and get some goals if necessary. Desperate for a chance. Still, he can only pick sixteen players and there are twenty-two of us sharing the same ambition. Game a nightmare for England. Bryan Robson dislocates his shoulder again. That's a big enough shock but immediately after Ray Wilkins is sensationally sent off by the Paraguayan referee for throwing the ball in his direction. Half-time brings urgent regrouping of forces. It's vital England don't lose the match. Ten men perform marvellously in second half. In fact, chances to win the game. But we know a goalless draw is not the best result for England. Main thing is we are still in there with a chance. We have to beat Poland next week or we'll be on our way home. Bit nasty as we board team bus to return to Saltillo. Supporters disappointed. Shake their fists at players and throw Union Jack flags to ground. Mood among players is sombre. We cling to hope of beating Poland. Team meeting after dinner. Manager mirrors our own thoughts on the day. Floodlit tennis till 11.00pm with Barnesy and then bed.

Saturday, 7th June

8.00am call from physiotherapist Fred Street. Early start for a monastery situated at 7,500 feet. Idea is to acquire altitude acclimatisation for later in tournament. We are determined to beat Poland and qualify for last sixteen. Arrive at 10.00am. Training for players not involved in game against Morocco. Stayed for five hours. Returned to hotel for quick swim and settled down to watch Portugal v Poland on television. The game was vital to our chances of qualifying. Poland won 1–0. Now we know. If we beat them on Wednesday we will have done it. More tennis at night with Barnesy, Glenn Hoddle and Alvin Martin.

Sunday, 8th June

Call at 8.00am. Training in Saltillo. Great session. Returned to see Scotland v West Germany on television. Scots play quite well and take lead through a superb goal from Manchester United's Gordon Strachan. Germans starting to look good now. Equalised through Voller and in second half Allofs hit winner. Left for monastery again at 1.00pm. Barbeque laid on – very nice. Changed pace with a game of cricket. Visit cut short by heavy rain. Back to hotel by 4.00pm just in time to see the best game of tournament so far. Denmark were devastating in beating Uruguay 6–1. Finishing of Preben Elkjaer impressed me. He got hat-trick. Michael Laudrup gave a great display. What a good player he is. Dinner at 7.00pm and bed by 10.30pm.

Monday, 9th June

Early start for training at Universitario Stadium in Monterrey where vital game against Poland is to be played on Wednesday. The manager split the players into two teams of eleven and warned us not to read anything into it because the side which would face Poland had not been finalised. But I was not in expected eleven and felt very disappointed. I still had hopes but they were receding rapidly. After training, travelled to Cima club to say goodbye. They had been good to us. I had picked up a slight strain in training so returned to Saltillo for treatment. Dinner at 8.00pm. Played pool. Bed at 11.00pm.

Tuesday, 10th June

Wake at 8.00am. Trained at Saltillo. Spirit among the lads is marvellous. We all get on so well together. Two disappointing results certainly don't seem to have affected morale. Mr Robson refused to name the team until the day of the game. Light lunch. Pool final in evening. Gary Lineker, renowned snooker-player as well as goalscorer, beat Terry Fenwick from Queens Park Rangers by 3–2. Bed 11.30pm.

Wednesday, 11th June

D-day. Wake at 11.00am. Slept well. Team meeting at 11.30am. Mr Robson names team to play Poland. Peter Beardsley to partner Gary Lineker at the front. They did well together in a fine win over Russia before World Cup. Disappointment again for me. At least I'm a named substitute which is an improvement. Peter Reid replaces suspended Ray Wilkins and Steve Hodge in for Bryan Robson. Trevor Steven also called up in tactical switch to four man midfield. Leave for Monterrey at 1.30pm. Even getting used to tight security now. Spirit among team tremendous. All aware of importance of game to England. What a performance! Poland destroyed in first half. Lineker hits hat-trick. Five man move started by Glenn Hoddle brings first goal in eight minutes. Second goal even better with Kenny Sansom, Beardsley and Hodge laying it on for Lineker. Hodge has one disallowed for some reason. Lineker wraps it up after thirty-five minutes after goalkeeper makes mess of Trevor Steven corner. Six minutes from time I replace Lineker. World Cup starts for me at last. Get in good position and believe I will score but ball doesn't come. England fans dance victory conga on terraces. Great atmosphere. England qualify in second place in Group F. We must go to Mexico City to meet Paraguay in last sixteen. I'm pleased I got on pitch. Seventh cap for me. Would have been great to have scored. Players bubbling on coach back to Saltillo. Dinner at 8.30pm. Applauded by hotel staff. Will be sorry to leave Saltillo. They've been good to us. Party atmosphere. Small party provided by Umbro. Everybody happy. Bed at 11.30pm.

Thursday, 12th June

Wake at 9.00am. Acclimatisation time again at the monastery. Played tennis. Stretching and jogging exercises to music – Fred Street's idea. Return to hotel at 2.00pm for lunch. Pouring with rain. Packed bags for Mexico City. Dinner at 7.00pm. Bed 10.00pm.

Friday, 13th June

What a day to travel! Wake at 7.30am. Leave hotel 8.30pm. Flight to Mexico City delayed forty minutes. Leave Monterrey airport at 11.45am, arrive at 1.00pm. Journey to hotel almost one hour. First impression a let-down. After magnificence of Broadmoor Hotel and home comforts of Camino Real in Saltillo the Valle de Mexico Hotel is not too clever. Television channels all Mexican. Thank goodness for our own videos and books. Dinner 7.00pm. Barnesy, Chris Waddle, Chris Woods and I discover indoor tennis court next door to hotel. Play for two hours. Chase ball across court and, in trying to return, hit myself with my own racquet. Blood everywhere. Stitches needed for wound between my eyes. Horrified by thought of being out of contention for Paraguay game and fearful of manager's reaction. Doctor puts four stitches in wound assisted by the ever-dependable Fred Street and Norman Medhurst. Group of the lads gathered outside medical room. They have a good laugh at my expense. Feel a right idiot. Have to put up with jibes for a couple of days. Sought sanctuary of hotel bedroom. It could only happen to me. Friday the 13th as well!

Saturday, 14th June

Wake 8.30am. Want to phone home but calls to England difficult to get. Meet Mr Robson at breakfast. He, too, has a laugh at my expense. He's taken some stick in press during World Cup but has held up well. Says injury is just one of those things. Still feel an idiot. Try to phone home again – no luck. Training at the English Reforma Club which we used last year on visit to Mexico. Nice place, good facilities. After training doctor had to wash my hair while I held waterproof gauze over gash. Lazy afternoon. Told by locals it was rainy season and would rain at 4.00pm. Spot on. It poured down. Returned to hotel. Dinner 7.00pm. Watched films on video. Bed 11.00pm.

Sunday, 15th June

Wake 9.00am. Training at Reforma Club. Great session. Watched

Mexico qualify for quarter-finals with 2–0 win over Bulgaria in televised game. Great goal from Negrete. Rain again at 4.00pm. Belgium v Russia in Leon televised in afternoon. What a match! Best of tournament so far apart from our first half performance against Poland. Belgians shock us all by winning 4–3 in extra time. Dinner 7.00pm. Visit to cinema to see film 'Commando'. Bit far-fetched. Bed at 11.00pm.

Monday, 16th June

Wake at 9.00pm. Many of lads report lack of sleep once more. Noisy hotel. Decision taken to move to Holiday Inn which is supposed to be less noisy and better hotel all round. Training at Azteca Stadium. Arrived at 11.00am but pitch being repaired so have to wait until midday. Just being there brought back wonderful memories for me. Stadium in better condition than previous year. Much work done. It's best stadium I have ever played in that's for sure. Still need help with washing hair – Barnesy and Ray Wilkins doing great job and cut is repairing nicely. Still hoping to be named as a substitute for Paraguay game. Brazil smash Poland 4–0 for quarter-final place. They're starting to look good. I'm the kiss of death for any team when I back them with our 'bookies' Glenn Hoddle and Kenny Sansom. Wager Argentina v Uruguay will draw. Argentina win 1–0. Now we must play them if we beat Paraguay. Should be interesting. Return to hotel and pack bags for move to Holiday Inn. When we arrive at new headquarters Italian team, the previous holders, there. Many of them are moaning about being away from home too long. Not the greatest attitude when playing France the following day! Dinner. Best food since arriving in Mexico City. Watched film 'Delta Fox'. Bed early.

Tuesday, 17th June

Wake 8.30am. New training pitch closer to new hotel. Good pitch. As expected Mr Robson names unchanged team apart from Alvin Martin replacing Terry Fenwick who is suspended after two bookings. Work on set-pieces again. Five-a-side match. No substitutes named. Manager plans for possible penalty shoot-out at end of game against Paraguay. Practice session set-up. I take a few. Decide if I'm in a position to take one on big day I'm willing. Back to hotel to watch Italy against France on television. I back Italy. France win 2–0 with great finish from Michel Platini. Typical! Telephoned home. Morocco against West Germany in afternoon. I back the Germans. I'd given up again when surprise, surprise Germans clinch a quarter-final place with a free-kick goal from Matthaus in the last minute. Team meeting at 6.30pm. Manager names substitutes and I am not among them. Devastated. No time for personal disappointments – team's the thing. We have to win. Manager outlines his strategy for game. After dinner a racing evening. Peter Shilton and I are the bookies this time. Great night all round. Shilts and I win £10 each out of six races. Bed at 10.30pm.

Wednesday, 18th June

Wake at 8.00am. Slept badly. Left for Azteca at 9.30am. Arrive at 'Palladium' as lads have nicknamed it at 10.15am. View from the bench is restricted. Chris Waddle and I watch the game from an ITV commentary box along with Manchester United manager Ron Atkinson, Tottenham chairman Irving Scholar and Ray Wilkins. Atkinson goes on air to hit back at criticism of Glenn Hoddle's performance from panellists back home in England. He seems a good bloke. Another two goals for Gary Lineker. He's leading goalscorer in entire tournament now with five goals. A great achievement by a super bloke. Peter Beardsley gets our third goal. Would have fancied myself to score if I'd been playing. Now Argentina in quarter-finals. Mood is good among the lads. Return to hotel for lunch then Denmark against Spain. Spaniards produce great performance beating fancied Danes 5–1. Emilio Butragueno scores four for Spain. Now he's joint leading scorer with Lineker. I've backed Denmark! Dinner 7.30pm. Mr Robson praises the players for their performance against Paraguay. Given day off tomorrow. Few celebratory beers. Bed at midnight.

Thursday, 19th June
Wake at 9.00am. Uninterrupted sun-bathing at last. All players relaxed, confident and pleased with yesterday's result. Camaraderie remains first class. Shopping in afternoon with Terry Butcher. I'll be looking for goals against him when we return to club football! Speculation about his future at Ipswich. Didn't find what we were looking for in shops. Returned to hotel at 5.30pm. Dinner at 7.00pm. Nice to relax for a change. It's been a long trip and we've worked hard. Bed at 10.00pm.

Friday, 20th June
Wake at 8.30am. Left for training at 10.00am. Tough session. Manager informs us this was the last hard day's work because games close together now if we beat Argentina. Lunch at 1.00pm. Visited by a boy called Fernando and his friends and mother. Lives in Mexico but a Chelsea fanatic. He'd contacted me as soon as arrived in Mexico. Gave him brochures and badges. He had a good time collecting all the autographs from players. Dinner at 7.00pm. Bed at midnight.

Saturday, 21st June
Wake 8.00am. Left for training at 'Palladium' at 9.15am. Informed couldn't train on pitch. Confusion. Waited one hour and then left to train at Atlantico Stadium. All locked up. Locksmith called for. He breaks into ground. Trained for just twenty minutes before returning to hotel. France v Brazil on television. France win match on a penalty shoot-out. West Germany also through to semi-finals. They beat host nation Mexico on penalty shoot-out. Fancied the Germans strongly in tournament. Dinner at 7.00pm. Team meeting. Manager names his eleven players for game against Argentina. Only change is Terry Fenwick back after suspension in place of Alvin Martin. More disappointment. Not among named substitutes. Feel very downhearted. Another racing evening. Shilts and myself along with Gary Lineker are the bookies. We clean up. Bed at 10.30pm.

Sunday, 22nd June

The big day. Wake at 8.00am. Leave for Azteca at 9.45am. Again I watch from ITV commentary box. Azteca full, awesome sight with supporters creating fantastic giant wave by standing up in sequence with arms in air. Diego Maradona handles ball to put Argentina in front. Very controversial. Then perhaps best goal I have ever seen from the best player I have ever seen. Chris Waddle comes on for Peter Reid whose had trouble with ankle. The Barnesy gets on with quarter of an hour to go. I'm chuffed for him, willing him to do well. He responds. He's brilliant. Argentinians are frightened to death of him. Fabulous cross gives sixth goal of tournament to Gary Lineker. That will make him top scorer in World Cup. I'm pleased for him too. He's a natural goalscorer and a hell of nice bloke. Barnesy is still going like a bomb. Last minute another great cross. Gary goes for it. It looks like he must get equaliser. He's bundled over and danger is cleared. England are out. All players sad. No doubts in our minds we would have gone further if we had got that equaliser. Return to hotel. Dinner at 7.00pm. Mr Robson tells us we have been a great squad both on and off the field. It's been a long haul all right. None of us would have missed it for the world. Had a few beers in evening with players, manager and some of the press guys who had been with us since Colorado. Bed at 1.00am. It's all over.

Monday, 23rd June

Leave for home at 8.05am. Much to reflect upon. Newspapers at home will be full of Maradona. Much discussion among players on way home about game against Argentina and World Cup in general.

Looking back I remain proud and privileged that I played a part in England's 1986 World Cup campaign. I'm sure there will be some people who believe all the hard work, all the dedication, all the absence from my home environment was a stiff price to pay for just six minutes of competitive action. But that's not my attitude at all. Representing your country must be regarded as the highest honour for any sportsman and throughout the World Cup I was a member of the squad of twenty-two players attempting to win the trophy for England. The disappointment experienced by seasoned players like Trevor Francis, Tony Woodcock and Dave Watson when they were left out of the final party must have been massive. And what about my Chelsea colleague David Speedie? He had been as pleased as punch when he had been led to believe he would be in Mexico representing Scotland. What a huge blow it must have been to him when the squad was announced and his name was not among the chosen few.

No, I had my six minutes of World Cup football and I will cherish them forever. George Best my great idol, Ian Rush, the goalscorer I admire above all others, have been unable to secure an appearance in the World Cup Finals. You can bet your last peso they would have willingly swopped places with me. Just being there will I am sure have assisted me in my ambition to become a better player and an even more prolific goalscorer. I was able to study at close quarters the finest exponents of the sport in action. I was also able to appreciate the quality of player on offer to the public in England week-in and week-out.

Peter Shilton is a goalkeeper I have always rated extremely highly. Now I know the secret of his success. His work-rate and routine in training sessions is absolutely phenomenal. He's exhausted at the end of it. He's just as much upset at being beaten in one of those sessions as he is in front of a full house at Wembley. The England players always believed that Shilts was the best in the world. He proved it in Mexico.

Chris Woods, who has subsequently joined Rangers from Norwich City in a new British transfer record for a goalkeeper, is also rated and appreciated by the England players. He too revels in hard work and concentration. He'll do well in Scotland, no doubt about that.

Peter Reid has signed a new agreement with Everton since the World Cup ended and I am not surprised that Howard Kendall was so keen to keep him at Goodison Park. If ever there was a natural leader on a football field it is Reid. He has a forceful personality which comes out on the field of play. He came into the team following the suspension of Ray Wilkins and despite being troubled by an ankle injury he imposed himself immediately. The Everton players in the England squad – Gary Stevens, Trevor Steven and at that time Gary Lineker – look to him for example. Peter Reid doesn't let anybody down. In the game against Poland he was encouraging everyone. At half-time when we were three goals clear the great Polish international Zbignieuw Boniek urged him to calm down, telling him England had won the match. Nobody cons Peter Reid. His first tackle, hard but fair, in the second half was on Boniek. He'll not thank me for reminding him that he's reached thirty years old now but, although he might not look a spring chicken on a football field, no team will be beaten easily with Peter Reid in their ranks.

The absence of Bryan Robson because of a further sad dislocation of his troublesome shoulder counted heavily against England. The captain is a genuine world class player and no team can afford to lose a player of such calibre. The England players were full of admiration for the way he battled on, refusing to return home for the vital operation to pin the joint. Within two days of dislocating the shoulder against Morocco he was training with us again and insisting he could play if required. Robbo certainly doesn't lack courage and his uncanny ability to produce match-winning goals might have made all the difference against Argentina. None of us will forget the sensational volley he produced to save our faces in Israel earlier in 1986. But then if Robbo had been available England would not have been celebrating the exciting emergence of Aston Villa's Steve Hodge. He had a super World Cup and is a certainty to become an established international in the future.

But the main star of England's World Cup bid has to be Gary Lineker. After a superb first season with Everton during which time he scored forty goals and was on target in the FA Cup Final against Liverpool he went on to beat the best in the world. Gary is an absolute natural who, I believe, can score goals in any company. Our paths first crossed when Gary was in the Second

Division with Leicester and my career was just beginning at Reading. We both attended an Addidas award ceremony having won the 'golden shoes' for being top scorers in our respective divisions. Ever since I arrived in the First Division after signing for Chelsea, I have been aware that Lineker was one of my great rivals to finish as leading scorer. In the 1985-86 season there was just no one to touch him. When he damaged his wrist playing for England against Canada in Vancouver in a World Cup warm-up match there was a genuine fear that he might be ruled out of Mexico. He didn't score in the opening couple of game but demonstrated his worth with three superbly taken goals against Poland and followed up with two more against Paraguay. He was a marked man against Argentina, yet still collected a goal which made him the top goalscorer in the entire tournament – an honour he thoroughly deserves. Immediately after the World Cup he joined Barcelona for a reported £2.8 million transfer fee. It sounds a lot of money but Lineker will be worth every penny and Barcelona have made a great buy. Goals are hard to come by in Spanish and Italian football, but Lineker will manage it. So, too will Ian Rush when he eventually joins Juventus. Great goal-scorers like these two just cannot be stopped.

Confidence plays a major part in the art of goalscoring. I had been determined to exert as much pressure as possible on Mark Hateley for the number nine shirt and when he got three goals in a pre-World Cup practice match I believed I could do equally as well. In the second half I went on and scored three goals as well. I have always believed I can get goals in any company and that belief has not wavered despite the fact I played for only six minutes in the World Cup. I believe that if I had been able to force a way into what was a very good England side I would have been among the goals.

There is absolutely no criticism whatsoever implied against the England manager Bobby Robson. He knows the game and his players and now has the invaluable experience of one World Cup under his belt. His selection of the squad to compete in Mexico was absolutely first class. All of the players got on well together and there was not a wrong word in almost two months, which is definitely saying something when a group of men eat, drink and work together for so long. The manager, along with his backroom team of Don Howe, Fred Street, Norman Medhurst and, of course, the devoted Dr Edwards, worked tremendously hard to ensure England's success. The preparation was first rate with not even the minutest detail left to chance. The result was a place in the quarter-finals – the last eight – and that cannot be rated failure by anyone's standards. It was said that changes were forced upon the manager because of injury to Bryan Robson and the suspension of Ray Wilkins and yet some time previously he had revealed in a newspaper article exactly what he would do if such a situation arose!

I am sure all of the squad will be delighted that Bobby Robson is to continue as the manager of England. We will all be better professionals for our World Cup experience. There are many good players in England and I am certain a strong challenge will be launched to capture the European Championship in 1988.

For myself, I'm determined to keep up the fight for a place in the England team, It won't be easy to achieve. An extra dimension in attacking strategy has presented itself with the success of the diminutive strike force of Lineker and Beardsley and it's no longer a question of getting the upper hand on Mark Hateley or keeping Luton's Mick Harford at bay. All I can do is carry on living up to my strengths and my main claim to fame – goalscoring.

FOOTBALL DAFT

I was born on 24th July, 1961 with the sound of an excited football crowd ringing in my ears. Our Victorian house in Oak Road, Luton was right next door to the Kenilworth Road ground of the local football club. My Dad was a professional footballer at Luton Town at the time, but I don't think he got more than one game as a centre forward before we moved on. Dad changed around a lot playing for Coventry City and various non-league clubs before we eventually ended up back at Luton at a house in Bodmin Road. I was almost three years old then and we were to live in this house until I was eighteen.

The earliest memory I have is of kicking a ball with Dad out in the back garden. He showed me how to head a ball, kick a ball, control a ball and keep a ball up off the floor. I was football daft, which I am sure absolutely delighted him. Other kids were into aeroplanes, tool kits, cars and all kinds of toys, but I never had them and never wanted them; I was happy with a ball. Running was my other athletic strength and Dad encouraged me all the way. However, my great passion then, and remains to this day, was the thrill of scoring goals.

Since my birthday is in July, a month before the start of every school year, I was always just that little bit younger than most of my classmates. Nowadays I'm a big lad standing six feet in height and weighing around thirteen-and-a-half stones but, as a boy, I was slight. In fact between the ages of eleven and fourteen my mother reckons I didn't grow at all. But I was a determined little so-and-so who just couldn't stand the thought of being beaten at anything and to this day I possess a ruthless, competitive streak.

When I was ten I went to the Beechwood Junior School. The previous leading scorer in the school football team had managed thirteen goals in just over twenty games and my first priority was to make my mark by beating that total. I achieved my aim within a month. In fact I went on to score sixty-six goals as a ten-year-old. All of us in the school team thought we were brilliant as we beat everyone in sight both in Bedfordshire and in London. We reached the Premier Cup Final, full of confidence, but were in for a rude awakening, being beaten 5-0 by Forest Green of London.

Dad was there. He hardly ever missed a game and doesn't miss many to this day. More often than not Mum would be with him and she comes along regularly now, too. They used to say they liked to keep an eye on me and nothing has changed.

I was also playing for a Sunday league team called Dunstable Claymores, a junior team masterminded by a good friend of my Dad called Brendan McNally. Brendan had played professional football with Luton and was to make a major contribution to my eventual success as a professional player.

At the age of eleven I moved on to Challney Secondary School and joined Luton Boys Club to play my Sunday football. I could not have been happier. It was there that I met up with Les Harriott and Mick Justin, who to this day remain my closest and most valued mates. It was football all the way for us three. Les and I were selected to play for Luton Town schoolboys team. There were a lot of good players in that team and, although I scored loads of goals, I wasn't the star by any stretch of the imagination. Some of the lads had the big clubs like Arsenal and Newcastle looking at them every week.

My Dad would come to watch every game, of course, and he made a point of keeping away from the various managers of the teams. He would encourage me as much as possible but would keep a low profile which I appreciated, because at times it was embarrassing to see how some Dads would push their own kids. The lads themselves didn't like it mainly because it would lead to some almighty ribbing from their teammates.

Looking back life seemed a procession of laughs and jokes and continuous football. We had great times and of course it's the good times you remember most of all. I was one of the lads and perfectly content in an environment of camaraderie and good fun. But I can remember being a bit of a moaner on the football field and I'd have a go at the other lads when they were not doing too well during a game. I suppose that had a lot to do with being ultra-competitive and wanting to win every match. I am still the same – ask David Speedie at Chelsea. We moan and groan at each other throughout every game. Off the field I am different altogether, as is David, but in our early days together at Chelsea our desire to win sometimes caused problems between us and culminated in a major confrontation.

There were few problems and no confrontations during my schooldays. I was daft about sport and the whole of my early life was dominated by competitive action. At Challney School the year was split into three distinct sections. The first term was devoted totally to rugby with soccer in the second term and athletics in the spring and summer months. I was a decent competitor in all three sports. I played in the fly-half position at rugby and was accomplished enough to earn a trial for England Schoolboys. But it was my mate Les who captured all of the glory and was the top scorer at that game. He played at number eight and was a big strong lad, who would literally smash everyone out of his way. I tried to get in on the act with my running ability and accurate kicking. I'd get the ball and run with it and sometimes I would pass grudgingly to a colleague, but nine times out of ten I'd attempt to go all the way and get a try.

Much as I enjoyed the diversions of rugby and athletics, football remained my one true passion. As a Luton boy I would try and watch Town play whenever possible. I saw the club through their days in the Fourth, Third and Second Divisions and it delights me that they are faring so well in the First Division these days – except when they play Chelsea of course! There have been many fine players connected with Luton Football Club: Malcolm Macdonald (a great goalscorer of course), Viv Busby, Brian Lewis, Jimmy and John Ryan, John Aston, Bruce Rioch and a good deal more. Jovial Harry Haslam was the manager in those days and the club seemed to receive a great deal of publicity due to his excellent press relations.

However, most of my time was taken up with playing the game rather than watching it. Yet, for a lad with such an all-consuming passion for football I am forced to admit that on reflection my attitude in preparing for the sport was not all that it might have been. It seemed I was more interested in the laughs and jokes with my mates than in the hard training required. It's not that I missed any training sessions but I know in my heart of hearts I didn't put as much into it as I could have done. I had to pay the price for my dilatory attitude when I was fourteen and a regular member of the Luton Schoolboys team. I had scored plenty of goals and, although there was one particular lad called Chris Jarvis pushing for my place, I was the one who was always selected. Mr Dave Morton was the teacher in charge of the team and on one occasion he arranged a training session to begin a little later than usual. It was a Friday evening when I usually went down to the Boys' Club disco with my mates. After a training session called at the normal time I would be home by 6.30pm and would then visit the disco until 10.30. Even though on this occasion the training time was a little later than usual, there would have been no problem in conforming with my normal Friday night arrangements. My mate Les and another pal Wayne Turner (who later played for the full Luton team and captained Coventry City) thought nothing of fitting in with the later training time but for some inexplicable reason I took umbridge at the disturbance to my cosy existence and told the lads to provide some suitable excuse for me. I had never missed a session before and thought there would be no problem this time.

How wrong I was. The lads returned from training and told me that Mr Morton had been outraged by my attitude. They had been instructed to convey the message that I would not be welcome in the team again. I was dumbstruck. My mind was in turmoil. I didn't know if Mr Morton meant it or not but I was about to find out that he was deadly serious. My reaction was, I suppose, typical of a teenager at a difficult age. I couldn't see that Mr Morton was right and that I was ridiculously in the wrong. I didn't go to training with Luton Boys anymore – and Mr Morton didn't bother to ask me to attend either. I'd put on a brave front when Les and the boys taunted me by telling me they were in this cup final and that cup final and concentrated on playing for Challney School at either football or rugby. But I missed my football with Luton Schoolboys terribly.

They played in one cup final against Hackney Schoolboys. I desperately wanted to go and watch the match but my pride just wouldn't allow me. My defence was to try and take the mickey out of my mates and I'd make derisory comments and say that Mr Morton had finally succeeded in assembling all of the creeps and crawlers. It was sour grapes on my part and nothing more and I'm not proud of myself for my juvenile reaction, but perhaps it was all part of growing up. Everyone makes mistakes but it's the man who learns from those mistakes who comes out on top. I wish I could report that my attitude improved because of that experience but many more years had to pass, which included other disappointments, before I began to really see where I had been going wrong.

There was nothing wrong with my form on the field of play though. The goals continued to pour in. Challney School swept all before them as we won every trophy there was to win. If there were four cups to compete for we would capture three of them and perhaps lose a fourth in the final.

In Sunday football I decided to move from Luton Boys to the Lewsey Centre team in the Chiltern League. I wanted a new challenge and someone had mentioned to me that a really nice bloke called Ron Fullbrook was in charge. I had an interview with him and was immediately impressed by his manner. Ron is a wonderful character and we remain friends today. That season was the happiest I spent as a schoolboy. Ron looked after us like a mother hen. I spent quite a bit of time socially with the boys of the Lewsey Estate as sometimes I attended discos down there, and many was the occasion when I'd knock on Ron's door at 10.00pm and ask him for a lift back to my own home which was about four miles away. He never let me down.

The rivalry between my old mates and me intensified when the Luton Schoolboys team got together and decided to enter a side in the Sunday league, calling themselves the 61 Club. My relationship with the lads remained friendly on a personal basis but there could be no room for sentiment on the football field. I concentrated on persuading my best mate, Les, to join us. He was a splendid centre half as well as a loyal pal and in the end he agreed but the decision caused quite a fuss. 61 Club protested and blocked the transfer for a while but eventually he was able to play alongside me for Lewsey Centre.

We finished third in the league and were runners-up in some of the cup competitions. I represented the County of Bedfordshire as well, scoring around 150 goals that season. It was a marvellously enjoyable, competitive time. If I'm honest I would have to admit that I was trying hard to get my own back on Mr Morton as I could not forgive him fully for kicking me out of the Luton Schoolboys team. There was to be no fairytale ending though – 61 Club finished one place higher than us in the league.

My Dad took the games very seriously indeed. If I'd played well and popped in a couple of goals all was peace and harmony in the Dixon household. But when he thought I could have done better he kept me in nights as a punishment. My sister Jane was a great sport. Sometimes she'd be waiting for me to come home and way-lay me before I could get into the house. Anxiously she'd ask: 'Did you score? Did you play well?' If the answer was no her face would fall and she'd say: 'Oh God. I don't want to go inside the house.' Dad has mellowed a bit now. We still have our arguments all right but he's my greatest supporter and my greatest critic all rolled into one . . . and he's rarely wrong. He's never been a man to pull his punches with me and appreciates that I have got to top the hard way, but insists there can never be any room for complacency.

Goals have always been my game. As a schoolboy I regularly scored four or five times in a match. On a few occasions I scored eight goals and once managed thirteen goals in a 16-1 victory. Right from the start I was always the top goalscorer in the teams I played for and the only time I can remember lagging behind was in my second season with Reading (my first season as a full-time professional player) when I scored only twelve goals. Neil Webb, later involved in big-money transfers to Portsmouth and Nottingham Forest, beat me with fifteen goals. I am very proud of the records I have achieved throughout my life. There have been a few people who have accused me of greediness when it comes to scoring goals and I admit I have always been single-minded in that direction. On one occasion when I was playing for the cub's team, a junior branch of the scout movement, I had scored something like thirteen goals in a game when they made me take over as goalkeeper to keep me out of the way. I didn't like it because when I've scored a goal I want to get another; when I've got two I want three . . . and so on. As a professional my outlook has remained exactly the same. I am not a man to ease up on anything, and with the setbacks I was soon to experience this quality above all others was to determine that I would eventually make it as a professional footballer.

REJECTED AND DEJECTED

Every schoolboy harbours a dream of what the future might bring. Some pursue the arts or the sciences, others fantasise of fame and fortune within showbusiness. I wanted to become a professional footballer. No other thought ever entered my mind.

From the age of eleven I had been visiting Luton Town Football Club for training and coaching sessions. David Pleat, the highly respected manager now in charge at Tottenham Hotspur, was the reserve team coach at Kenilworth Road back in those days. A coach called Danny Bergara, was in charge of the promising schoolboys. The two men were as different as chalk and cheese. Mr Pleat struck me as an extremely serious, studious type of man who attempted to instil solid professional habits into his pupils. Danny, much more the extrovert, loved to witness outrageous skill on the ball. He was a Uruguayan by birth and a happy, flamboyant personality who delighted in watching players do tricks with a football. Mr Pleat, on the other hand, encouraged tight discipline and was pleased with players who worked hard at their game. They provided an almost perfect combination as far as encouraging and educating schoolboys in the rudimentary basic philosophies of the game.

My ambition was to progress through the ranks to play for my home town team. I didn't manage to get into the Youth team on a regular basis at first because they had some outstanding players on their books. A lad called Godfrey Ingram was the shining star. He had amazing skills and looked destined to enjoy considerable notoriety as a professional player, but Ingram became yet another example of the maxim that there is no such thing as a certainty in football. He went to America from Luton and later joined Cardiff City but precious little is heard of him these days. Another fine player of that time at Luton was Phil Driver who went on to join Wimbledon and Chelsea. Luton Schoolboys and the Bedfordshire County team formed the nucleus of the Luton Town Youth Team and the younger players, like myself, got their chance when the older apprentices were called upon to play in the reserve team.

I'll never forget one bizarre occasion when I had been named as substitute for that Youth team. With twenty minutes remaining in the match I was sent on and can recall touching the ball only once when Mr Pleat and Danny Bergara decided to make another substitution. I couldn't believe it when I realised that I was the player to be pulled off. The substitute was being substituted after only five minutes! I was flooded with a potent mixture of shame, anger and bewilderment. I couldn't believe this was happening to me. As usual my Dad was at the game, standing on the touchline. I walked over towards him, crying and confused. He tried to console me but he, too, was in a daze because he just couldn't think of a reason why a fifteen-year-old boy should have been treated so harshly. We stood together until the end of the game and then Dad instructed me to go and shower and change with the rest of the team. I felt sick inside. I didn't speak in the dressing room. Nobody spoke to me either. To this day I cannot understand why I should have been pulled off after just five minutes of play. I reported for training, as usual, the following week and when the team was announced for the next match I was no longer down to be substitute. I had been named in the side itself.

I ended that season as the leading goalscorer for the Luton Youth team. I didn't play in all of the matches and I cannot recall exactly how many goals I got, but I do know it was a hell of a lot, which was very satisfying for me especially after the way I had been treated in that one game. I don't suppose Mr Pleat or Danny Bergara would remember the incident now, but to my dying day I will never forget it. I have never been so humiliated in my life. There could be no possible excuse for treating an impressionable young player in such a shabby manner. It was a shattering experience. Maybe they were not happy with my attitude and I appreciate now that it left much to be desired in my younger days. I had a couldn't-care-less air about me and always attempted to get by on doing just enough. Once again I was to pay a high price for my short-comings in that direction.

We used to do our training with Luton Town after school in the evenings. Shortly before the spring half-term Mr Pleat told us that during the school holidays we were welcome to report to Kenilworth Road if we felt like it on Tuesday, Wednesday and Thursday. I turned up on the Tuesday and Wednesday and as Thursday was the last day I thought I'd done enough for one week. It was a half-term holiday after all and I wanted to do other things. There was no game on the Saturday in any event. I joined my mates in watching the first team play on the Saturday afternoon and was waiting for a bus with my mate Les after the match when Mr Pleat came walking by. He spotted me immediately and asked where I had been on the previous Thursday. I blustered a hasty reply saying I'd had to go out with my Mum. Mr Pleat muttered something about being able to go out a lot more with my Mum next year and moved on. I didn't think much more about the incident but the implications of what he had said were always at the back of my mind.

About six weeks later the club began to issue the registration forms to the players they had chosen to keep on as apprentices. One by one the lads were called to one side and assured they would be signed by the club now that their schooldays were coming to a close. All of us were looking for a job of work to do. I'd considered nothing but professional football. The Youth team had provided a healthy crop of players for that year. We were an outstanding side. Only two players failed to attract the prized apprentice forms . . . Kerry Dixon and a close pal called Johnny

Mawhinney. I was devastated. The usual defensive barriers were erected in my mind. I tried to make out I was a big shot who couldn't have cared less. What a joke. The feeling of nausea just wouldn't go away. Mum and Dad were supportive, but Dad was never a man to go in for platitudes and false consolation. Straight from the shoulder he told me perhaps I wasn't good enough after all. His words didn't provide much comfort but neither of us could see any other explanation.

I enjoyed the summer despite the feeling of numbness at my failure to be accepted by the club I had always wanted to play for. I received a letter from Luton informing me that, while they had believed at the time it was the correct decision not to offer me apprentice forms, they were willing to sign me as an amateur so they could play me in their teams on a Saturday if they needed me. They invited me down to Kenilworth Road for a chat but I couldn't really see any point in wasting my time. By chance I bumped into Danny Bergara in the street and he told me not to feel too downhearted and to take inspiration from Ricky Hill. Ricky, a player I rate very highly who has since played for England, had also been denied apprentice forms and had made the grade as an amateur. Danny admitted that Luton's judgement might prove to be wrong in the long run and tried to persuade me to sign on as an amateur in the hope I would improve as a player in their eyes so that I could be signed on a professional basis. I declined the offer even though I was desperate to join Luton. My pride would not let me stoop so low as to grovel my way in as an amateur. No, far better I told myself to get it out of my mind and accept I just wasn't good enough to become a professional footballer.

Dad advised me to get a job and play football in my spare time. At this time Brendan McNally was manager of Chesham United in the Isthmian League. I went along to train with them and to hopefully find a place in their reserve team. I was just sixteen years old and looked upon as no more than a confident whipper-snapper but Brendan had great faith in my ability. He had played for Luton Town as a full-back in the 1959 FA Cup final against Nottingham Forest and he knew what he was talking about. He was aware my inner confidence had been damaged by my failure to be accepted by Luton as an apprentice and picked me as substitute to the first team at Chesham on several occasions. I was aching to get into the action and finally I got my opportunity.

Chesham were 4-1 down in an away match at Hornchurch when Brendan decided the time had come to pitch me in. He took off the regular centre forward Jim McCarthy with twenty-five minutes of the match remaining. Jim didn't like it one bit and stormed towards the touchline flinging his shirt on to the floor in a gesture of disgust. Gordon Taylor, the assistant manager at Chesham, was playing in midfield. He told me not to worry and just to play my normal game. Shortly afterwards Gordon scored and then I popped one in to make the score 4-3. We were in full flow now I can remember the sheer excitement of hitting the equaliser. Just before time one of our lads smashed in a winner. The great elation felt at such a memorable comeback was heightened by the fact that at just sixteen I was to become a regular member of the team. The goals continued to flow and Jim McCarthy soon realised that he'd lost his place, perhaps forever, and switched to the centre half position. He became a most accomplished centre back and I was later to play in the same team with him once more at Dunstable.

As I adapted to the team and the Isthmian League, my form improved dramatically and I was getting better as an all-round player. On leaving school with a couple of O' level certificates and CSE passes, I had taken up an apprenticeship with the local firm of Cardale Engineering as a toolmaker. It was a hectic life what with work, college and football, but I enjoyed it all in those early days and took everything in my stride.

A major moment in my life occurred when a work mate of my mother's said he could arrange for me to have a trial at Tottenham Hotspur. Maurice Walby was as good as his word and it was not long before I had scored a goal for Spurs in a 3-1 win. Peter Shreeve, who went on to become manager of the club, was in charge of the reserve team and helped Ron Henry with the youths. John Mawhinney, rejected with me at Luton, was also given a trial and the Tottenham management said they had been impressed with us both.

The team was involved in a cup final, played over two legs, against Oxford United. Neither John nor I played in the first game which Spurs lost 4-1 and there didn't appear to be much chance of pulling the tie around. But I was picked to play alongside lads like Mark Falco (who went on to make a name for himself as a striker at Tottenham), Gary O'Reilly (now at Brighton), Giorgio Mazzon (Aldershot) and Gary Brooke (Norwich) and my mate John played up front alongside Falco and I. The entire team produced an inspired performance and I scored two goals in a 4-0 victory. I knew I had played well and was very pleased with myself.

Tottenham were sufficiently impressed to offer me apprentice forms and it was time for another serious talk with my Dad. I was approaching the age of seventeen and had been lucky enough to be taken on by Cardale as an apprentice. Dad was worried I would have just one year to convince Tottenham I was good enough to be taken on as a full-time professional and pointed out that if I left my job and gave up college I would have nothing left to fall back on in the event of failure. Together we decided against accepting Tottenham's offer. Peter Shreeve was marvellous saying he understood my decision and applauded me for being sensible. He said he was prepared to make me a part-time professional so I could still play for Spurs even though I remained an apprentice toolmaker. All was agreed so long as Cardale Engineering were amenable to the idea. The bloke in charge of the apprentices was called Mick Burrows, whose kindness, patience and understanding has played no small part in my success as a professional footballer. He could so easily have put the block on the arrangements because it meant I had to leave work a couple of hours early to be sure of catching the train to get me to White Hart Lane on time. To make up for the lost time I had to work late on other nights.

There were many exciting games in that memorable year with Spurs. We won the South-Eastern Counties League and I collected over thirty goals in the season. The only sad note was my mate John was released by the club half-way through the year. It was a tough, exhausting life. Dad would pick me up in his car from work to rush me off to the railway station. I would then travel to London and catch a tube train to Seven Sisters before walking to White Hart Lane just in time for a training session at 7.00pm. Ron Henry was in charge of the training but Peter Shreeve was always in close attendance. Sometimes we'd catch a glimpse of the manager Keith Burkinshaw and his assistant Pat Welton, as well as the great Bill Nicholson who was scouting for new players following his magnificent career as a manager when he won the League Championship and FA Cup double.

Ron Henry was a super fellow. He used to give me a lift back home to Luton when the training was completed. He was a real Londoner who told great stories of his exploits with the double winning team. I was happy with Spurs: the dressing room banter was lively and the players were great lads who fostered a marvellous team spirit. But the nervous part of the season was approaching when players were to be told whether there was a future for them at Spurs. All of the conversation was geared to asking 'Have you heard anything? Well, have you heard anything?' One lad called Jez Reardon cleared off to America. Whether he couldn't stand the suspense I don't know, but it provided a pleasant surprise for me a couple of years ago when I was visiting Los Angeles with the England team. Somebody came up to me and said that Jez had asked to be remembered. It seemed he had settled comfortably in America and was a successful businessman. It just shows that people don't forget in football.

Meanwhile, all the players were becoming more nervous and irritable and still I had heard nothing about my future. I had already begun to fear the worst when one night after training Peter Shreeve told me he wanted a private word. He said he had bad news. He didn't need to say any more but I'll never forget the way Peter Shreeve handled a very delicate, traumatic moment in the life of an ambitious young man. He explained that Tottenham were not going to take me on as a full-time professional and revealed that at Spurs the policy was for a committee to reach a decision on the future of a player. Keith Burkinshaw, Pat Welton,

Bill Nicholson, Ron Henry and Shreeve himself had taken their vote on Kerry Dixon . . . and Kerry Dixon had lost. Shreeve stated gently that I had presented one of their most difficult cases. I remember his words as though it was yesterday: 'As yet we don't know about you,' said Shreeve. 'We feel we are not prepared to take a chance. It was a split decision. The manager was forced to exercise a casting vote. I would like you to know that Ron Henry and I wanted to take a chance with you. We have seen the most of you. You have scored a lot goals and we believe you could score those goals in the reserve team.'

The fact I was approaching my eighteenth birthday obviously counted against me. It meant, of course, I would be too old to qualify to play in the Youth team and, although I had already appeared a couple of times for the Tottenham reserves in the Football Combination League, the competition for places would have been intense. There just happened to be an abundance of quality strikers at Spurs during my time with the club. Consider the names: Peter Taylor, the forward who went on to play for England; Gerry Armstrong, a fixture in the Northern Ireland international team for years; Colin Lee, now a colleague of mine at Chelsea; Ian Moores, a big strong, strapping player who did well in the First Division; Chris Jones, a more than useful performer who also enjoyed success in the Tottenham senior team. Fellow youngsters like Mark Falco, who has now become a first choice striker at White Hart Lane despite the purchase of a string of expensive players during the past few years, was, I suppose, my most direct rival. Coming up very quickly from behind was Terry Gibson, rated as the best of all the young players at Tottenham at that time. He was eventually sold to Coventry for just £90,000 by the then manager Keith Burkinshaw and when Peter Shreeve took over he tried to buy him back. Gibson eventually moved from Coventry to Manchester United in the 1985-86 season for £350,000. Peter Shreeve carefully explained that if they had signed me as well it could have created an impossible situation. The club would have been in a position where professional players were not getting a game each week. I was desperately disappointed and, I must admit, terribly confused. There I was, the most outstanding goalscorer in the Tottenham Youth team, being told I was not good enough to continue playing for the club, and the fact that there were just not enough places to accommodate all the players was no consolation. Shortly after succeeding Burkinshaw as manager at White Hart Lane Shreeve was quoted extensively in the newspapers as to why I had been allowed to leave the club. Shreeve said: 'Had I possessed the managerial power I have now, Kerry Dixon would still be with the club and leading our First Division attack alongside Mark Falco. I thought he had done more than enough to merit being signed on a full-time basis by the club. But others did not share my belief in him, unfortunately. He has matured into a young man who has literally got the world at his feet. There are no targets he cannot attain. Provided he stays clear of serious injury I think we are going to see him scoring goals at the highest levels for the next decade.'

I will never forget Peter Shreeve for his kindness, understanding and consoling words to a young player whose ambition had been shattered. I have always been able to relate to people who are honest and straightforward with me and I've discovered there are a lot of two-faced people in the football profession but Mr Shreeve was certainly not one of them. All of the young lads at Tottenham respected him. We regarded him as something special. He dedicated his life to Spurs and did a magnificent job through the ranks, finally achieving his great ambition when he was appointed manager of the club. Sadly, he failed to live up to Tottenham's expectations but I hope they will not forget the very special talents which got him there and the massive debt they owe to him. All too often, in my opinion, a good, decent, talented man is allowed to leave the club just because it is felt he has not quite come off as a manager.

Yet no amount of consoling words from Shreeve were able to heal the pain when Tottenham no longer required my services. As usual I turned to Dad for advice and he was adamant that I should persevere with my engineering apprenticeship. I knew that he and Mum were disappointed for me but they didn't allow themselves to show it. To be honest there had been no guarantee I would have accepted Tottenham's terms even if they had been offered. I had long since convinced myself in my own mind that I should complete my apprenticeship. But I wasn't allowed the opportunity to choose . . . and that's what hurt. I considered myself lucky to be in a position to have a job to fall back on and I realised, as much as anyone else, that with unemployment figures rising I was fortunate to have a trade. I was studying for a Technical Education Certificate in engineering, mathematics, pure mathematics and all of the sciences. In short, I had to master the theory behind the practice and my parents urged me constantly to work hard because a qualified toolmaker was the highest paid worker in the factory. They insisted I would appreciate my good fortune later in life and of course they were proved right, as parents so often are.

I was earning the princely sum of £28 a week which meant that after the normal stoppages I had about £22 left to bring home. Ever since the first day I was given a pay packet Mum had taken £5 off me each week for what she called bed and board. In fact, she put every penny of it into a bank account for me. I had no choice in the matter but I didn't mind one bit. The following year she withheld £10 from my wages and this, too, went into the bank account. Whenever we had an argument she would tell me the money she'd taken was all hers but she couldn't fool anyone. Her little exercise provided a lesson in the value of money which I practise to this day. My earnings these days are a far cry from the £28 a week I started with but the same basic values remain with me. I'd been earning £30 a match from Tottenham as a part-time player and this coupled with my wages from the factory, which had by then risen to £35 a week, enabled me to believe I was doing very well for myself considering I wasn't yet eighteen.

I absolutely hated the factory life and it was the football which had helped to sustain me; now that had been taken away. When it began to sink in that I would not be going back to Spurs, the thought that I was just not going to be good enough to earn a full-time living as a professional footballer made me dreadfully depressed. This was the second time I had been rejected despite scoring winning goals on a consistent basis. Maybe I just did not possess what it took to make it. Yet this was the last time in my entire life that I allowed myself such thoughts – Kerry Dixon would make it.

THANK EVANS FOR READING

Although my dream of becoming a professional football star appeared to have been shattered I was still determined to play the game at the highest possible level. Once again it was time for a heart-to-heart talk with my Dad and his unequivocal advice was to stay calm and not rush into anything. I had received an offer from Orient to go on their summer tour. It seemed my reputation as a goalscorer had encouraged them to give a trial but perhaps it was just as well that I was unable to accept because I was working full-time in the factory.

Mr Shreeve had assured me he would do everything possible to help me and shortly afterwards Charlton, one of his former clubs, made me an offer. In truth, though, I was slightly disillusioned with professional football. Making the grade was no longer the be-all-and-end-all of my life. Deep down I had not abandoned all hope of proving Luton and Tottenham wrong in their judgement but had adopted the attitude that if I was not going to make the grade it was important for me to face up to it. I have a remarkable capacity for being able to shut things away in the back of my mind and was happy leading my ordinary life and enjoying to the full socialising with my mates. However, my love for the game itself had not diminished in the slightest; the real problem was where and when I could play. Fortunately, a situation presented itself which was to make my decision a formality.

Brendan McNally, who had been manager of Chesham when I played there, was appointed manager of Dunstable Town. The club had been upgraded to the Southern Premier League in the re-organisation caused by the introduction of the new Alliance League, even though the previous season they had finished in the bottom half of the Southern First Division. I was happy to negotiate a deal with Brendan but my arrival barely caused a ripple of excitement. The big news was that Dunstable had been able to sign a player called Stuart Atkins who had been the leading scorer with Wycombe the previous season. In fact, I knew Stuart well and had played in the same team with him at Chesham. He'd scored more than 200 goals and Dunstable paid a then club record fee of £1,500 to Wycombe for him.

What a partnership we proved to be. It was goals, goals and more goals. My Dad had been a regular player with Dunstable some time before but even he was forced to admit this was the best team they had assembled in years. We were on top of the Southern League by Christmas and eventually finished the season in sixth position. When the Southern League Select Eleven was chosen neither Stuart nor I were included which was a big disappointment to say the least. But I got a late call when someone dropped out through injury and it wasn't long before Stuart was playing alongside me for the Southern League team as well as Dunstable. We played representative games against the Isthmian League, Northern Premier League and the Alliance League. In the final play-off we captured the representative title with a 2-0 win on the Dulwich Hamlet ground, Stuart and I getting the goals.

In my first, and what was to prove to be my only season with Dunstable, I finished as the top goalscorer in the entire league with fifty-two goals, and Stuart a close second with thirty-seven. What a memorable time it was. There was tremendous camaraderie at the club, creating an atmosphere I will never forget. I always went to the Tuesday and Thursday night training sessions. The belief in my own ability, which had been almost totally destroyed by both Luton and Tottenham, was now restored. I was perfectly content to remain with Dunstable. It became a standing joke in the dressing room that all kinds of professional clubs were looking at me. There was even speculation that Luton were preparing to swallow their pride and sign me and Torquay made a definite bid of around £3,000 but Dunstable resisted the temptation. Everything had gone right for me at Dunstable from the moment I played my first game for them in a pre-season match against Luton reserves. I enjoyed that one all right. David Pleat was there watching and my mate Les was at centre half against me. In fact all of the old pals I had known at Kenilworth Road seemed to be playing. We won 2-0 and although I didn't score I was well pleased with the result.

Dunstable played their matches on a Saturday afternoon and I would work all week in the factory and enjoy a night out with the lads on a Friday, nothing too heavy, perhaps a disco. I didn't drink alcohol in those days so there were no problems in that direction. But I can recall one painful experience particularly well. One Saturday morning I got back a little bit late. In fact, it was 3.00am as I approached the house I lived in with my parents. Mum and Dad had always been strict on discipline and the worst punishment as a youngster for any misdemeanor was to be confined to the house for a week. My parents could exercise physical punishment as much as they wanted but I hated being confined to barracks. I would concentrate on being a good lad for a couple of days and then try and sneak my way back into Mum's affections and when Dad came home from work I would chat him up for a while. He knew what I was up to but would grant me permission to go out until 10.00pm knowing full well that the disco I was attending always finished at 11.00pm. If I protested he would suggest I didn't leave the house at all. It felt so hard at the time but as a parent I would act in exactly the same way and my respect for my parents will never weaken. But on the night I returned from the disco at 3.00am I was in a state of panic. I tried to sneak up the stairs but the light snapped on and Mum was standing there with a face like thunder. She went absolutely bananas with me: 'Where do you think you have been?' she demanded. Before I could reply there was a stinging slap across my face and she then proceeded to read the riot act: 'You have a game tomorrow, young man,' she raged. 'You are letting everybody down and you just don't care, do you? It's high time you got a grip on your life,' she went on. 'You are a disgrace. It's time you became a lot more responsible instead of thinking about nothing but discos and hanging around with your friends. Your Dad has given up on you.' I was dumbstruck. Such is the ignorance of youth that I had believed I was doing nothing wrong. I wasn't a boozer, I had a job, I trained two nights a week, I played football every Saturday and in general had never done anyone any harm. Mum had shocked me all right. I couldn't forget the venom in her face and in her tone.

The following afternoon I played for Dunstable and we escaped with a draw. I was feeling aggrieved at my Mum's words of the previous night and thought I was hard done by. None of my mates seemed to have to put up with that kind of nonsense. But even then, in my heart of hearts, I knew she was right. I knew the proper preparation for a football match at any level was not disco-dancing until 3.00am and I was also aware that my unprofessional attitude had played a major part in my failure to establish myself at both Luton and Spurs. Looking back from a position with Chelsea and England, I am very much aware that without parental strength and guidance behind me I might not have made it. The greatest thrill of all now is the knowledge that I provide my parents with so much enjoyment. They share my hopes, anxieties, ambitions and dreads and have instilled in me that life must be lived for the moment. My Dad smashed his knee cap in a game at Southampton and he never forgets to remind me that injury can end a career in an instant. I still spend most of my time with them. The money I have earned from football has enabled me to buy a lovely house of my own; that is my security and hopefully I will have enough money to pay the mortgage off by the time I have finished playing football. But my home is, for the moment, with them.

Everything was going well for me at Dunstable when, out of the blue, I was told that the club had accepted a bid from Third

The pleasure of scoring my first goal in the First Division is obvious as I find the net against Arsenal at Highbury, August 1984.

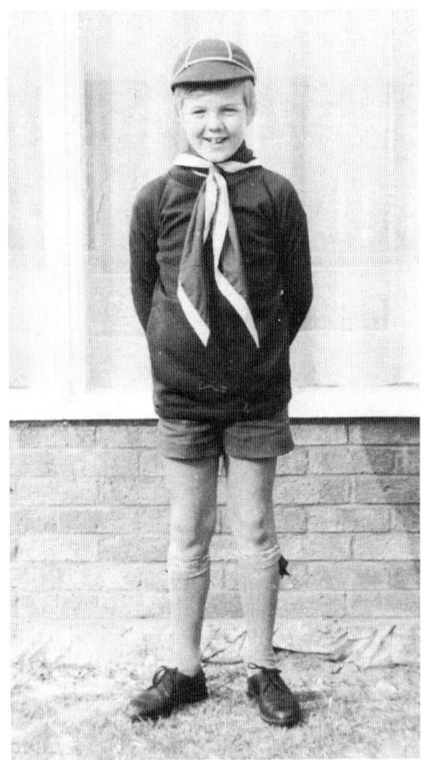

TOP LEFT *All strikers have to learn to walk before they can score – my first tentative steps under the guidance of Mum.*

TOP RIGHT *The best part of being a cub was playing in the football team. I scored so many times in one match they made me go in the goal.*

OPPOSITE PAGE BOTTOM *I always hogged the ball, even as a youngster. Here I am (centre) with my pals off to play our favourite game.*
ABOVE *The Dixon family: Mike, Ann and my sister Jane. Without their support I would never have made it as a professional footballer, let alone to Mexico.*

RIGHT *I sign for Reading, with assistant manager Stewart Henderson supervising the arrangements.*

BELOW *I was lucky enough to get among the goals quickly when I first joined Reading.*

Chronicle

TOP *Ball's eye on the ball as Alan watches me score against Pompey.*
BOTTOM *Eye on the ball like all the textbooks say. This was against Portsmouth.*

CATHAY PACIFIC
GUINNESS

OPPOSITE PAGE TOP *I have missed a few penalties in my time but this one beats QPR 'keeper Peter Hucker.*

CENTRE . . . *and it's time for relief.*

BOTTOM . . . *and then celebration.*

LEFT *Watford manager Graham Taylor almost signed me from Reading, but here I help Chelsea to a 3–1 win over Taylor's Watford in March 1985.*

BELOW *My World Cup teammate Viv Anderson of Arsenal tries to mesmerise me into giving the ball away.*

TOP *A thumping goal in September 1985 against my home town team Luton on their artificial pitch.*

BOTTOM *My pal Glenn Hoddle comes out second best in this aerial challenge.*

Division Reading. I wasn't at all excited by the possibility of becoming a full-time professional but after a discussion with Dad we agreed we should meet with them out of courtesy. We met the Reading manager, Maurice Evans, at a pub just off the M1 motorway. He struck me immediately as a warm, friendly, honest man. He was also extremely persuasive and after a while I began to warm to the idea of giving it a go again. He stressed that although Reading was an ambitious club, they were making no guarantees on a place in the team, but he believed that with a few reserve games behind me I would be good enough to play in the Third Division. I was about to enter the final year of my apprenticeship at the factory and I knew full well that things might not work out for me at Reading. I was determined to resist the temptation to sign for Reading as a full-time professional player. I was approaching my nineteenth birthday and realised the decision would be vital to my entire life and career. I explained my predicament to Mr Evans and he was most sympathetic. Between us we agreed a two-year contract which would enable me to play as a part-time professional for the first season so allowing me to complete my apprenticeship with Cardale Engineering. The major obstacle was it would be impossible to do my training with Reading in the evening because there would be no one at the ground. It was imperative that a way was found for me to get to know the other players otherwise we would have met only on match days. I sought advice from Mick Burrows at Cardale who agreed to me taking two mornings a week off work so long as I reported back to the factory by 2.00pm on each occasion and made up for lost time by working until 6.00pm every day. It was another fine gesture from him and the deal with Reading was finalised.

This was the first time in the history of Dunstable that they had been able to sell a player directly to a Football League club. They were happy enough with the fee as well: a handsome profit indeed for a club which deserved every penny of the reported £20,000 and a just reward too for Brendan McNally, whose faith in me had never wavered. Time and time again he'd told me that one day I would become a full-time professional footballer and a mighty successful one at that. I recall telling the local newspaper on the day I was leaving Dunstable: 'My aim is to be in the Reading first team in time for Christmas although there can be no guarantee. If I do make it, and can stay in the team for the rest of the season, I will believe I have done well.'

I was amazed when I was selected for all four of Reading's pre-season games and not even a 5-1 thrashing from Luton in a friendly affected my enthusiasm. But I had not scored a single goal, although the manager backed me in the local newspaper by saying he was sure I would, once I had settled down. He added that he had not expected me to challenge for a place in the team so early in my career at Reading but he intended to give me a run. In fact, I played in the first twenty-five games of the season and it came as quite a bombshell when I was dropped from the team. From then until the end of the season I was in and out of the side spending most of my time as substitute. Perhaps it did me good, perhaps I had been expecting too much too soon. In any event I played in the last ten games of the 1980-81 season and produced a flurry of goals to establish myself as the top goalscorer in the club. My first ever goal in the Football League came against Brentford on 23rd August, 1980. Reading won by 2-1 at Griffin Park and I am sure the goal will hardly be recalled by anyone but myself and my nearest and dearest. It was a simple tap-in, but the pride and excitement I felt will stay with me forever. I could not have been more elated if it had been the winning goal in a World Cup Final and vowed there and then that it would be the first of many.

Being a part-time professional was in no way a satisfactory state of affairs. The lack of practice sessions with teammates was bound to affect cohesion, understanding and team work. I was also disillusioned with work in the factory as football had now taken over my life completely. I'd had a bit of success, scored a few goals, and that was all I could think about.

A new charge-hand had been appointed at Cardale and it wasn't long before I began to feel he was picking on me in particular. I didn't help matters because I set out on occasions to annoy him deliberately and a bust-up between us was inevitable. One morning he came over to me and screamed that as I had done nothing all morning I'd better get working and fast. I saw red. I told him, in the ripest possible language, to go away. It was an irresponsible error on my part. I was totally out of order but my common sense had been clouded somewhat by the bad relationship between us which had been simmering for some time. A complaint was made against me to the works' foreman and I was sacked on the spot. I was stunned. What made it worse was I had just eight more weeks of my apprenticeship to complete. The years of work and study were to be utterly wasted. I apologised profusely but in vain, and tried to explain I had acted in the heat of the moment against someone who had been niggling at me for weeks. But the foreman insisted the charge-hand represented him in the factory and that by swearing at him I had sworn at the foreman himself. The charge-hand was loving every minute of it. After six months of attrition he had caused me to snap and I was out. I had destroyed everything; all the work, all the studying, counted for nothing. I would have no alternative but to go out into the world as an unskilled man.

When I returned home and told my parents what had happened I was given a real rollicking. The only chance left was to make a personal plea to Mick Burrows, who by this stage had been promoted to works' manager. Dad came along with me and we explained the situation. Mick was hardly sympathetic and gave me a severe dressing down for my impetuous behaviour, but he admitted the foreman had acted extremely hastily in sacking me on the spot. So it was arranged for me to be transferred from the toolroom to the welding machines which was a bit of a punishment but nothing like as severe as dismissal, and allowed me to get my papers signed as a fully skilled toolmaker.

As soon as I had completed my apprenticeship the time had come to qualify as a fully skilled footballer. I realised that as a full-time professional my devil-may-care attitude just had to change. It was now or never for me. Football was to be my profession, my livelihood and I was determined to make a real go of it.

My Dad was also leaving nothing to chance. When I'd signed for Dunstable he had helped to soothe the pain of rejection by Spurs with words of advice and encouragement. Now he was laying the law down in no uncertain terms: 'This is your big chance to make a living out of the game,' he said. 'If you are going to do it, do it well. Your attitude must be nothing less than one hundred per cent from this moment on. It won't matter if you are not the highest paid player in the world. What is important is that you aim to become a top First Division player. If you can't achieve that, then aim at being a top Second Division player and so on. But just make sure you are good at whatever level you attain. It's a great life, go out and enjoy it. You'll have your fair share of fun but make damned sure you give it everything you've got. It beats working in a factory all of your life. Whatever you earn be sure to keep something back to rely on. The price of failure will be high. You'll spend the rest of your life haunted by what could have been achieved if you had been dedicated. Work at the game, want to win, want to succeed.' I listened intently and thought deeply about what he was drumming into my mind. I was nineteen, not a child any more, my destiny was in my own hands. That will to win, that desire to succeed no matter what the obstacles has carried me a long way.

In the initial stages of my first season as a full-time professional I suffered grievious misgivings. I had expected to go from strength to strength after finishing as top scorer with Reading as a part-timer and believed that the full-time training would make me fitter, sharper and more experienced. I'd completed the previous season with five goals in the final seven games and became anxious and concerned when the goals refused to flow at the beginning of the 1981-82 season. The pre-season could hardly have been described as successful as far as I was concerned. I have always been a notoriously slow-starter as it takes me time to capture my timing and rhythm, but at the beginning of the 1981-82 season I was experiencing more difficulty than usual. In fact, it was all a bit of an anti-climax because far from the spectacular entrance to full-time professionalism I found myself in the reserve team. I worked harder than ever before to capture the attention of Maurice Evans and was burning with ambition and commitment but my naivety was exposed both on and off the field.

I had first been confronted with the hard facts of professional life shortly before my twentieth birthday in July. I was approached by a reporter named Russell Kempson who worked for the local *Reading Evening Post,* who said he was looking to write a piece that would mark my birthday and the fact I was about to embark on a full-time career. He suggested it would be a nice idea for me to set a goalscoring target of twenty for the season to match my age. I remember thinking and possibly saying that twenty goals would indeed be satisfactory in my first full season. The headline in the newspaper next day knocked me sideways: 'I want a goal for every year,' it proclaimed. I cringed with embarrassment, it sounded so boastful, so crass. It had not meant to sound like that at all. I don't blame the reporter concerned one bit as it was very much my own fault. The reporter was looking for a nice line to go with his story but in cold print I had been portrayed as a loud-mouth who had become too big for his boots. That's not me, that's not my style and never will be. The incident provided a precious insight into the manipulations of the media men and I had been taught a lesson I would not forget in a hurry. From then on I was careful about what I said to the newspaper reporters and thought I had mastered the art until I was confronted by the experienced Fleet Street operators. They really know how to angle a question so they will have a story no matter what the answer. It can be very difficult to come to terms with the knowledge that every word you say can become headline news, but at least for a while I had learned to avoid the temptation to put myself on a pedestal. Yet, throughout the season there were to be repeated reminders of my irresponsible boast. Soon the match reports, written by the same Russell Kempson, were claiming: 'Dixon, who pledged to score twenty goals this season, doesn't look like achieving the target.'

The emerging star of the Reading team at this time was Neil Webb, a midfield player of considerable ability. Scouts from all over the country were despatched to examine his capabilities. It was a hard first season for me, yet I completed it with a flourish scoring a total of twelve goals in forty-four first team games – only three behind Webb. This is the only time in my entire career to date when I have failed to be the leading goalscorer with my club. In the final game of the season we won 2-1 at Gillingham and I played well. I had begun to feel much more comfortable with the pace, technique and technical skills required in the Football League.

By this time my two-year contract with Reading had expired and there had been little sign of the club offering me a new agreement. I was not earning a fortune; in fact, I could have picked up equally as much money if I'd continued as a toolmaker and played in non-league football. My basic wage as a full-time player was just £120 a week with bonuses of £40 for a win and £20 for a draw. If we were beaten, which was hardly heard of, then we got no extra whatsoever.

There has never been a time when I have regretted the route I had to take into the Football League. Most players progress to the professional ranks after negotiating the schoolboy and apprenticeship scheme, but so many of them end up rejected and on the dole when it is too late to take up another skilled trade. My pal Les was a great example of this kind of thing happening. He was an apprentice at Luton with me and, while I was rejected as a professional, Les was offered terms. He played regularly for the Luton reserve team but when he had reached the age of twenty he was released and has been in and out of work ever since, playing non-league football to keep his head above water. In contrast, my professional career was just starting when I was twenty.

However, I was beginning to get the feeling that Reading were not too bothered about offering me a new agreement. On reflection, it is obvious they were waiting for the players to report to the club for the start of the 1982-83 season, but after a couple of days' pre-season training no negotiations had been forthcoming. I was in no hurry to go anywhere and there had been no dispute or anything like that. The situation changed rapidly when, out of the blue, I received a telephone call from the Gillingham manager Keith Peacock, who said he would like to meet me for talks with a view to signing me for his club. We met at a London hotel and I found him a very likeable sort of person, full of enthusiasm and optimism about the future of Gillingham. He insisted that with me scoring goals in their attack they could make excellent progress and offered me a basic wage of £220 a week – a full £100 more than I was earning at Reading – and to me that sounded like a fortune. Mr Peacock admitted it was a lot of money for a club like Gillingham to pay a player and I told him I was willing to sign. I was a free agent and there was nothing to stop me except the great respect I held for Maurice Evans. It would mean I would have to move out of my parents' home but Gillingham would be paying me enough money to compensate. Gillingham understood I would have to talk to Maurice Evans about the transfer and they insisted they were more than willing to allow an Independent Tribunal to settle a suitable transfer fee. There was no way I would have signed for anyone without discussing it with Maurice first as I was aware of my responsibility to him. I would not have been given my break in top class football had it not been for Maurice.

A lot of managers had come to take a look at me when I was playing for Dunstable but Maurice was the one with the courage of his convictions. He had backed his judgement and invested £20,000 of Reading's money in a non-league player. The transfer could have cost him his job if I hadn't done well. He was playing for high stakes. He had become a friend and a major influence on my life and career. Even when he chose to drop me from the team he was full of encouragement and words of confidence about my ability to make the grade in the Football League. I think he was a bit taken aback when I told him I intended to sign for Gillingham. He asked me what they were offering me and then instructed me to join the rest of the players for training while he had discussions with the Reading chairman. When I'd showered and changed after the morning session I was called in to see Maurice again and immediately offered a new contract which was worth more than £20 a week in basic pay to what Gillingham had been prepared to give me. I was taken aback. In one stroke Reading were now willing to double my previous pay.

I didn't really want to leave Reading. The club had been good to me and I believed I was learning my craft with them. My main concern was in disappointing Mr Peacock. I asked Maurice for his advice and he told me the ball was in my court, saying either I signed for Reading or moved to Gillingham. There could be no in between. He stressed he wanted me to remain at Elm Park and believed passionately that I had the ability and the ambition to play with distinction in the First Division. The least I could do was share the faith Maurice so obviously had in me. I was very embarrassed by the conversation with Mr Peacock when I telephoned him. I explained Reading had made an excellent offer to stay with them and that I genuinely believed I was in their debt after they had taken a chance with me from the Southern League. He was charming and admitted he had expected Reading to put up a fight to keep me at the club and accepted my decision, having the good grace to wish me every success. My decision was to herald the start of a successful season for me personally, but it ended in trauma and failure for Reading Football Club.

The opening games brought steady rather than spectacular results but I was happy enough with my individual game. I'd scored four goals in the pre-season friendlies and five in two Football League Trophy matches, including a hat-trick against Aldershot. The first Third Division game was at Bradford City where we lost 3-2. It was a memorable day for me because I scored a goal at the end of a long run from the half-way line. I produced another two in the second game against Plymouth and made it four in the opening three games of the season with an effort which gave us a draw against Brentford. The *Reading Evening Post* provided a special feature but this time there were no ridiculous quotes from me. The article did, however, illustrate that my name was becoming known in the game: 'Despite Reading's uncertain start to the season there can be no doubting the ability and potential of their young centre forward Kerry Dixon. He is already attracting the attention of several senior clubs including West Brom, Newcastle and Aston Villa. This season he looks ready to explode upon the Football League scene. He is the ideal build for a striker and looks stronger than at any previous stage in his career. There are still a few rough edges to his game which can certainly be smoothed out with expert coaching. It is his blistering pace which is the vital asset and he makes most Third Division centre backs look ponderous. Young Kerry will definitely play a major role in the destiny of Reading during the coming months. If his promise is fulfilled he could well become as talented a centre forward as any in the division and the club's saviour in more ways than one.' The article gave me a lot of pleasure, not only because I wouldn't have been human if I hadn't appreciated the nice things being said about me, but because I had learned it was better to allow others to shout from the rooftops.

I rapidly began to realise the 1982-83 season might become the most important of my entire career to date although, unfortunately, the team was not doing at all well. A good illustration of the mixed fortunes for Reading and Kerry Dixon was provided by a game at Doncaster on 25th September, 1982. It was a day I'll never forget. I scored four goals, but Doncaster smashed in seven beating us 7-5, and the club had slumped to 22nd place in the table. Maurice Evans described the game as: 'The most amazing match I have seen in thirty years of involvement with football. It could have been 12-12.' In fact, it had been a day when the whole of football seemed to have gone goal crazy: Watford thrashed Sunderland 8-0, Luton drew 4-4 at Stoke, Southampton lost 5-0 at Liverpool and Ipswich smashed six goals past Notts County. There were plenty of other four and five goals spread around the League, and that day a total of 201 goals were scored in the English and Scottish Leagues – the most for twelve years.

My four goals received tremendous coverage in the Fleet Street newspapers but I retained a very low profile in what I said to them even when it was pointed out I was the first player for twenty-four years to score four goals and end up on the losing side. Nevertheless the scouts from the big clubs had got the message and they began to converge on all of Reading's games. Manchester United, Nottingham Forest, Arsenal and many more were mentioned but significantly the names which cropped up most of all were Watford and Chelsea. John Neal, a long-time friend of Maurice Evans, was the manager at Chelsea so it was no surprise that he was a regular visitor to our Elm Park ground. Maurice was forever being quoted on the fact that I would be a big name player in the future with a reputation for scoring goals at whatever level. Words like: 'Anyone from the First Division who doesn't gamble on Kerry is absolutely crazy. This is only his second season as a full time professional and he can score goals in any company,' poured out of Maurice.

It certainly didn't do my growing reputation any harm at all when we confronted First Division Watford at the quarter-final stage of the Football League Trophy. I scored in a tremendous 5-3 win which brought my goal tally for the season to twenty-three in just twenty-five matches. The game had gone into extra time and was one of the most exciting I have ever played. We were 3-1 down with just ten minutes of normal time remaining but came back to 3-3, and I claimed our fifth goal in the extra period. But this time it wasn't just the goal which had thrilled me the most. I knew I had played one of the best games of my life.

It's amusing now to look back and recall that Maurice immediately changed his tune about a possible transfer for me to a First Division club. Watford manager Graham Taylor observed: 'Dixon is tremendous. Every time he got the ball he looked dangerous. He has played like that every time I have seen him. How do they manage to keep hold of him.' My crop of goals had established me as the leading marksman in the entire Football League and Maurice began to insist publicly: 'He's not for sale, no way.' I wasn't upset in any way by Maurice's remarks. I was happy enough at Reading learning my trade, practising my craft as a goalscorer and I knew my chance would come soon enough to move to a First Division club so long as the goals didn't dry up. I had become a target for the autograph hunters when we played away from home. It felt strange to be asked to sign my name on a piece of paper and, in fact, I used to get down-right embarrassed about it. I can remember thinking that some people must be very easily pleased. Perhaps it was a natural mental reaction because I had never considered myself to be anything special or out of the ordinary. I still don't. Of course, I am much more comfortable now with the people who ask for my autograph and I consider myself honoured they should ask me at all. At this time I was approached by two journalists, who lived in Reading, offering to look after my business affairs and personal publicity. Brian Roach was involved in the publicity department of the Rothmans cigarette company and Roger Ware worked with the *Daily Mirror*. They explained their plans suggesting a fan club be started and personal appearances organised. I didn't really see what harm it could do and was all for it. I met Brian's family and he met mine, they were nice people, and to this day nothing but good has come out of our relationship. He arranged for a newspaper column to appear in the *Reading Evening Post* under my name for which I was paid a small fee, providing the first money I had ever earned from football for outside club activities.

Everything seemed to be going extremely well, apart from Reading's position in the Third Division, which was giving increasing cause for concern, when, out of the blue, I slipped on some mud in a game just before Christmas 1982 and overstretched. I didn't think too much about it at the time and played in another two games before beginning to notice a problem with the muscles in my groin. I began to stiffen up after matches; before long the pain was beginning to affect me before the end of matches and I was struggling to complete the full ninety minutes. Slowly but surely the situation deteriorated. Soon I didn't dare sit down at half-time or I wouldn't have been able to get back up again. I couldn't run properly, my movement had become seriously restricted, and it wasn't possible for me to partake in any form of training or physical exercise during the week. I spent every day in the treatment room before hobbling off the table to try and play in the games on the Saturday.

At the start of January 1983 the situation had become extremely worrying. The physiotherapist at the club, Glenn Hunter, who is still with Reading, said he had seen a similar kind of pelvic problem before and that I should consult a Harley Street specialist. I took his advice and underwent what seemed to be hundreds of X-rays in every conceivable position before I was given a verdict. I was told I had a pelvic problem which wasn't serious in the long-term, but would continue to cause considerable pain and discomfort unless I was prepared to rest completely. Dr Nigel Harris warned there was no way the condition would clear of its own accord and I was ordered to stop playing football for at least a month. On my way to Harley Street I had been dreading such advice but when it had been spelled out to me in such graphic terms I was willing to do anything to clear up the trouble. I had become frightened that the injury could threaten my entire career. Nevertheless, it was an extremely difficult time for me as it was the first major injury I had experienced. I did exactly as instructed but became totally dejected as Reading were losing matches while I was just a helpless bystander.

Towards the end of the month I tried to begin a slow build-up to a comeback; nothing strenuous, just gentle walking and a bit of exercise. I returned to the specialist in a confident mood because the pain had ceased and, to my great delight, he pronounced the all-clear but cautioned me to make slow progress with a lot of physiotherapy. Believe me, I had no intention of rushing anything. The injury had frightened me out of my wits. I'll never forget the pain which had affected me under my buttocks and in my back, legs and stomach. After games I had been unable to pull up my own trousers in the normal fashion and was forced to sit on a bench and lift them slowly up to my knees. I couldn't lift my legs at all and had been unable to bear any exertion from the waist downwards. I'd been scared all right.

The welter of get-well messages and cards from supporters and friends certainly cheered me during a time of great mental stress and uncertainty. The response from the newspaper column was tremendous, as well as from the fan club, and I took great care in ensuring all letters were answered. The lovely Kathy Tayler, who had finished third in the world modern pentathlon championships, lived locally at Reading and she helped Brian Roach to form the club. She became member number 001 and helped to run the club itself until business commitments made it impossible for her to continue. We remain firm friends and she still takes a keen interest in my career. One letter I treasure was sent to me by a lifelong supporter of the club called Margaret Bainbrigge. She had been a season ticket holder at Reading since the war and had written a lovely poem for me:

Kerry the striker, a brilliant lad
The best goal ace we've ever had
Quick on the turn, great in the air
And never a tackle that isn't fair

Here's wishing you well and a speedy return
To the game that you love and to which the fans yearn
So here's to you Kerry, keep your chin up
Who knows one day, you may win the Cup.

I was very moved by the poem and the thought that someone cared enough about me to sit down and write it. I went along to see Margaret at her home in Tilehurst near Reading and thanked her. She told me she had been keeping a scrapbook of newspaper cuttings and photographs of my career and promised that when I played my first game for England she would present it to me, which she indeed did.

After receiving permission from Dr Harris to begin light training again, I attempted some gentle jogging and spent a lot of time swimming. But another month had elapsed before I felt confident enough to suggest to Maurice Evans that I might risk a return to the team. There were about thirteen games remaining and Reading's plight was becoming increasingly perilous. From a personal point of view I was anxious to try and provide the goals which would rescue them from the Fourth Division and, at the same time, re-establish myself as the top scorer in the Third. Before the injury I had privately set my sights on smashing the all-time goalscoring record for Reading which was held by Ronnie Blackman having scored thirty-nine League goals in the 1951-52 season. I had begun to believe this might be possible after hitting twenty-one goals in my first twenty-two games of the season, but the injury had extinguished any such ambitions.

On the day before the team was due to play an important match at Cardiff I reported to Elm Park for a training session. I was aware I was not match fit and so there was no possibility of me playing at Cardiff, even though I had made up my mind to travel with the lads and lend some moral support. I was feeling pretty good and optimistic that it wouldn't be too long before I'd be back helping them out on the pitch. I kicked one of the training balls and the pain shot right through my body. I just couldn't believe it. I was dumbstruck. I knew what it was all right; the pelvic problem was back. I don't think I have ever felt so despondent and was very much aware that the recurrance of the injury almost certainly meant I would be out for the entire season. The fact that when I got out of bed the next morning to join the lads for the coach trip to Cardiff the groin was not as sore as I had expected provided no immediate consolation. But what happened that day was straight out of a 'Roy of the Rovers' comic strip.

I'd been dubbed 'Roy of the Rovers' by the Reading fans when I met a Wiltshire publican named Tom Tully, who had written the comic book stories of Roy Race for three generations of Melchester Rovers followers. A story about the mythical Roy had appeared in the Reading club programme alongside a picture of myself and the fans latched onto it. I suppose it was all part of the image but I didn't like it and it was a bit embarrassing walking down the streets of Reading with people shouting: 'Look, there's Roy of the Rovers.'

I didn't much resemble Roy Race when I boarded the team coach for Cardiff that day, but within minutes the situation changed dramatically. Several of the lads were playing cards on the way down the M4 when Ken Price suddenly began to complain of a sore back. His condition worsened rapidly and the physiotherapist diagnosed the problem as a muscle spasm. There were just twelve players in the party plus coach Stewart Henderson and myself. I remember thinking that the obvious solution was to switch one of the players into attack and promote a lad called Mark White from substitute. Henderson would have to take over the number twelve shirt. The party stopped at a hotel for the pre-match meal and it was clear that Ken Price was by now in desperate pain. I jokingly suggested that I should make a shock comeback and everybody had a good laugh, but having formulated the idea myself I began to believe it was by no means impossible. I considered the facts: if I was back to square one with the pelvic injury I knew exactly what it entailed, aware that the groin would stiffen up towards the end of match and I would be in considerable pain the following day. It wasn't long before I had convinced myself I could do it. I went to Maurice and suggested he allowed me to make a comeback. I reasoned that as there were not too many matches left in the season, I could get through and take a complete rest in the summer. Besides, Reading's position necessitated the gamble. The manager was uncertain but promised to consider my suggestion.

The team coach travelled the final half-hour to Cardiff and, as soon as we arrived, Price was given a fitness test but we all knew he had little chance of playing. Maurice came in to the dressing room, looked long and hard at me, and said tersely: 'Get stripped.' I was so chuffed it was ridiculous. I was as happy as a little lad who has been told he is going to the circus. I went out with a spare football boot from one player on my left foot and another borrowed boot on my right. The Reading fans had travelled to the game in force and they went crazy with excitement when I walked out to play, and I remain convinced I would have scored in the very first minute if I had not been barged in the back just as I was lining up a header. That first minute challenge on me brought a penalty and I thought to myself that this really was 'Roy of the Rovers' stuff and I had better take it. But Stuart Beavon claimed the ball . . . and missed. Reading provided a good team performance that day and the point from a goalless draw was fully merited. I had been reasonably satisfied with my own performance although I had lacked my usual zip. The pain was there but not bad enough to convince me I shouldn't play out the remainder of the season.

The following day I had stiffened up but it was nowhere near as bad as it had been earlier in the year. However, it was not the real Kerry Dixon who fought to rescue Reading from relegation in the frantic end to the season. I scored five goals in the last eleven games which captured the 'Golden Boot' goalscoring award for the entire division but couldn't save the club from the drop. The scouts were back in force but the injury made it impossible for me to live up to my reputation.

D-day for the club arrived on 14th May, 1983. We had to win our game at home to Wrexham, while Exeter had to lose at Newport if we were to stay in the Third Division. The match at Elm Park kicked off fifteen minutes before the Newport v Exeter game and when I scored a goal there were high hopes we had been saved, especially when the news filtered through that Exeter were losing. The fans gathered on the pitch ready to celebrate our reprieve but a late goal from Exeter flattened our hopes and expectations.

It was indeed a sad day for the club after a season when, at one stage, it had looked as though the name of Reading would disappear forever. Robert Maxwell, chairman of Oxford United, had claimed he had acquired enough shares to ensure a merger with his own club to form Thames Valley Royals who would play in a new stadium at Didcot. The massive publicity afforded to Maxwell and the uncertainty experienced by the players, manager and staff of Reading Football Club cannot have assisted in the struggle to beat relegation. The fight for control at Reading spilled into the High Court with a local millionaire and former Reading footballer, Roger Smee, taking up the cause to prevent the merger. It certainly appeared that the supporters of both Reading and Oxford were totally opposed to the proposed plan. The arguments and counter-arguments carried over into the close of the season and, such was the uncertainty among the players, that just Ken Price and I were signed up for the 1983-84 season and only because we were already committed by contract. Brian Roach, who was working hard as my agent, helped to mastermind the counter-publicity campaign launched by Mr Smee and was later to become a director of the club. In the end, Smee won his fight to preserve the name and individuality of Reading but by then the new season was upon us.

My name began to crop up again as a transfer target for the big clubs and Mr Smee, who had taken over as chairman, immediately slapped a £200,000 price tag on my head. Rumours were fast and furious and I must have taken telephone calls from every football writer in Fleet Street. I was beginning to worry that I might be priced out of the market, but I trusted Maurice Evans implicitly and I knew he would keep me informed of any developments. I also knew that if I hadn't sustained the pelvic injury I would have scored a lot more goals and Reading might not have been preparing for the new season in the Fourth Division.

It was only much later in life that I discovered Watford were waiting to buy me once I had proved my full fitness. I was sharing a bedroom with Watford's John Barnes when we were on England duty. He took a telephone call from his Watford manager Graham Taylor who told John to pass on the message that the biggest mistake he had ever made was in not signing me when he had the chance. Mr Taylor had watched me playing when I was not fully fit at the end of that season and didn't think I was the same player he had admired in previous matches. He was right, of course, but he hesitated and lost the chance. My twenty-second birthday was approaching and Brian Roach, now a director at Reading, sent me a Watford scarf. I regarded it as the broadest possible hint that I would soon be on my way to Vicarage Road. The idea appealed to me because I would still be able to live in Luton close to my mates, as Watford is only just down the road.

The new chairman made changes in the backroom staff at Reading bringing in Ian Branfoot from Southampton as first team coach and assistant manager to Maurice, with Stewart Henderson demoted to Youth team duties. Branfoot made his presence felt immediately. He's a tough, dour man who made it clear from the start that he expected to get Reading out of the Fourth Division at the first attempt. The first ten days of pre-season training were absolute murder. We were all knackered at the end of it even though I had taken the precaution of a few cross-country runs of my own. The squad was split into small groups and Branfoot introduced himself to the players by running along with each of them. He was certainly incredibly fit for his age. He ran alongside me and said: 'You're Dixon aren't you?' I replied 'Yes,' there didn't seem much else I could say. 'I've heard a lot about you,' came the reply then he took off to the next group. I soon began to suspect he didn't rate me too highly. Then the club signed Trevor Senior from Portsmouth who had a reputation for goalscoring, and this transfer sparked another storm of speculation in the national press about my future.

Unknown to me negotiations with Chelsea had reached an advanced stage, though a report that Reading had rejected a big offer from the Stamford Bridge club disappointed me. I knew that when Maurice Evans was ready to tell me what was going on I would be put in the picture fully. It pleased me when Maurice came out with a statement in the press saying: 'There is little sense of loyalty in the game these days and most youngsters in Kerry's position would be agitating for a move. But he is happy to stay until we are presented with an offer we cannot refuse. It is a unique situation. Half of the clubs in the First Division have inquired about him. I am sure his exemplary character will prove to be a decisive factor in any deal.' Then, out of the blue, came the telephone call I had been waiting to receive. I was told a transfer fee had been agreed with Chelsea and I was to travel to Aberystwyth, where they were conducting their pre-season training, for talks on personal terms. I was elated but the euphoria was short-lived. Within half an hour Mr Smee was on the telephone to tell me the deal had broken down. Terms had been settled at £150,000 but Reading were demanding a further £25,000 if I was ever selected to play for England. I was told to report to Elm Park the next morning for training as usual. I didn't know where I was. My mind was in turmoil. At 8.00am the next day Mr Smee telephoned again to say I should need an overnight bag because the deal with Chelsea might be on again.

I was on my way and I knew it, but I'd been in no hurry to leave. Reading Football Club in general and Maurice Evans in particular had been good to me and for me. I will be forever grateful that they took the chance and gave me an opportunity to make a name for myself in professional football when I believed all was lost after rejection by Luton and Tottenham. I had enjoyed my football and my life with the club. I still go back there on a regular basis to watch their matches and perform promotional functions in the town. Reading's results are the first I look for on a Saturday night and I was delighted for all my old mates when they won promotion to the Second Division for the first time since 1958 at the end of the 1985-86 season.

Maurice Evans was a very influential figure in my life and I retain the utmost respect for him both as a manager and a gentleman. He has a marvellous eye for a goalscorer. He signed me from Dunstable, Trevor Senior to replace me and he helped sign John Aldridge who has performed some spectacular goalscoring feats for Oxford. It shocked me deeply when he was sacked by Reading when the club was in fourth position in the Fourth Division in the season following my departure for Chelsea. I sent him a telegram of commiseration and a letter of congratulations when he was appointed by Oxford United. I like to stand by the people who have done well for me. I wouldn't be where I am now if it wasn't for Maurice Evans and I remain in his debt.

STEP-UP WITH CHELSEA

Elm Park, Reading had rarely known such excitement. The chairman of Chelsea, the infamous Ken Bates, was due to arrive at the ground to pick me up and drive me off to Aberystwyth for pre-season training with the rest of the Stamford Bridge squad. Suddenly the buzz went round that Mr Bates had arrived. 'He's here, he's here,' came the shouts and whispers and in strode a slightly chunky figure complete with piratical beard. He was not at all what I had expected. In my mind's eye the picture was of a huge, physical man with a cut-glass accent. Reality had produced a loud, abrasive, super-confident bloke.

We were introduced and after a quick hand-shake he snapped: 'Right, let's go!' I had a feeling this was going to be a very interesting car journey. It was the first time I'd been near a Rolls Royce, let alone sat in one for a journey which would take almost five hours. The Bates Roller was green with sumptuous leather seats and plush carpeting which stretched up the inside of the doors. I felt a little uncomfortable at the outset, mainly because I didn't know whether Mr Bates wanted to talk about my personal terms immediately or wait until we had discussed the matter with the club manager, John Neal, at Aberystwyth. As the miles rolled by we talked about football and life in general and I realised that he had very quickly eased my anxiety and that I was in no way in awe of him. In fact, I'd taken an instant liking to the man. I respected his attitude to life and his general demeanor appealed to me. To be perfectly frank we got on like a house on fire. The hours and the miles seemed to fly by so compulsive was his conversation, when suddenly he said: 'Right, we've had all the bullshit, how much do you want to sign for Chelsea Football Club?'

I had previously sought advice from Maurice Evans on the kind of reasonable figure I could put to Chelsea. I hadn't a clue about the wages of First and Second Division players and suggested to Mr Bates the amount Maurice and I had decided upon. He became quiet for the first time since leaving Reading; but not for long. He reeled off a list of players' names he could have signed for similar wages and seemed to be aware of all the transfer movements within the game. He then switched the conversation to the length of contract. Chelsea wanted me to sign a four year agreement with them, but I preferred two years and after a bit of wrangling we compromised on three years. At no stage did he make me feel uncomfortable or inferior although I had begun to realise he was an extremely skilled negotiator. As quickly as the discussions had begun he brought them to an end, insisting the real talking would have to be done in consultation with the manager when we reached Aberystwyth. He was undoubtedly proud and excited about his plans for what he continually termed 'the new Chelsea'. He explained to me exactly why he had stood by the manager when all believed he would be sacked following Chelsea's appalling performance in the Second Division the previous season. The club had finished fifth from bottom of the League, just two points away from relegation to the Third Division for the first time in their history.

My immediate impression of Mr Bates was one of a man who enjoyed almost a perverse pleasure in proving other people wrong. The situation at Chelsea had been clear: either the manager had to go or the players had to be sold. The easy way would have been to sack John Neal but the chairman was astutely aware that to have dismissed the manager would have solved very little. He chatted excitedly and incessantly about the players who had already been signed by Chelsea during the summer of

1983: Joe McLaughlin, Pat Nevin, Eddie Niedzwiecki, Nigel Spackman and John Hollins as player-coach. To be honest I hadn't heard of half of them, though Hollins, of course, was well known following a distinguished career, and Spackman and I had played against each other, but as for the remainder I hadn't got a clue.

As we approached Aberystwyth I had the temerity to inform him that one day I would like to have a Rolls Royce to drive around in. He replied: 'If you help to make Chelsea Football Club great again then you might get one. I intend to take this club to the top and if you do the job for which you will be handsomely paid you will grow with us.' I was a bit troubled as to how I should address him in future. Should it be Mr Bates? What about Mr Chairman? The reply was typical of the man: 'Call me what you like, I don't care', he said. 'Make it Ken if you want.' So Ken it was until more than a year later Brian Roach heard me calling him Ken in conversation. Brian always made a point of calling him Mr Bates and was horrified. I explained to him that I had always called him Ken. He's one of the lads, down-to-earth, a normal fellow, a self-made man, but Brian's observation began to trouble me. I had always been comfortable in the company of the chairman but now I was avoiding calling him anything at all. Finally I asked him straight out how I should address him. He replied with a grin: 'You've always called me Ken, carry on, I don't mind.' It was agreed. Ever since then I have called him Mr Chairman! The car journey to Aberystwyth made an indelible impression on me. In fact, Mr Bates became a bit of a hero of mine and would be my example to follow as a man of achievements. I wanted a Rolls Royce and a similar lifestyle. Later I was to visit his farm at Beaconsfield, just outside London, and that was fabulous.

On our arrival in Wales I was introduced to Mr Neal plus Ian McNeill the assistant manager, John Hollins, Peter Bonetti and Gwyn Williams the Youth Development Officer at Chelsea. The players were staying in a youth hostel while the chairman was booked into a hotel. We all had dinner together and the chat was lively and the atmosphere particularly warm and friendly. John Neal struck me as a quiet, deep-thinking sort of character, proud of his no-nonsense Geordie origins. He didn't say too much at our first meeting and would answer my statements with words like 'champion' or 'that's canny, eye.' While the two clubs had reached agreement on the size of the transfer fee the real business of agreeing a suitable wage with me had yet to begin. After dinner the manager and the chairman slipped off for a quiet consultation before I was called over and discussions began in earnest. The chairman left me to talk things over with Mr Neal who suggested I might be asking a little bit too much. I told him that no matter what the outcome of our negotiations I would want to discuss the entire matter with my parents before reaching any final decision on whether to sign for Chelsea.

It was decided we'd leave it at that for the night and I was taken along to the youth hostel and given a room with instructions on the proceedure for the following day. All of the other players were in their beds when I got there so I didn't see anyone until breakfast at 8.30am sharp the following morning. I walked into the dining room and sensed all the players looking up to examine the possible new boy. I sat down at the end of a long table and lads like Joe McLaughlin and Chris Hutchins went out of their way to be friendly and welcoming. I was a bit apprehensive because I didn't really know what to expect from the training. I was very much aware that Chelsea wanted to see me in action before committing themselves to a definite transfer because of my injury at the end of the previous season. I convinced myself I would be all right since I was experiencing no problems with the pelvic injury and I had already completed ten days pre-season training at Reading. The Chelsea boys had been at Aberystwyth for only two days so I should have been in better shape than them. What a rude awakening awaited me.

The manager had a great belief in players beginning their build-up to the season on sand. The surface is not like grass or even concrete in that the sand pulls at the muscles and drains the energy. My eagerness to impress soon proved to be my undoing. At Reading we had taken the mickey out of the apprentices because they never seemed to pace themselves as they'd fly around the opening lap of a race in about forty seconds, taking 140 seconds for the last one. What an idiot I was. I charged into the first circuit around a sand dune while John Neal stood by, stop-watch in hand, and it wouldn't have been so bad if my time had been exemplary but it was only average. As soon as I stopped running my legs began to wobble and seize-up, and I collapsed in an untidy heap on the sand. A short breather was allowed before the players were split into teams for a relay race over the top of the dunes. I picked up the baton, charged up the sand which slithered away from my feet and eventually hit the top of the dune. I was clawing at the sand, desperately fighting for some kind of hold. My head was spinning, my lungs at bursting point and my legs completely without feeling. How I managed to get over the top of that dune I will never know. I collapsed into a pathetic heap once more as I fought the overwhelming feeling of nausea. I thought I was going to die. All of the lads were pointing at me and laughing hysterically, they thought it was wonderful to see their highly-priced new boy struggling for his life. If I'd been in their position I would have done exactly the same. What the hell had I let myself in for. Never in my whole life had I experienced anything like it. Somehow I managed to do it all over again but my legs were moving from memory and, just when I thought the agony was over, we were instructed to complete a run along the beach which stretched for more than three miles. I was panic-stricken. I had always been absolutely hopeless at any kind of long-distance running and even at Reading I was always close to the back of the pack. What chance would I have alongside these super-fit athletes? My legs felt as though they had gone missing anyway. We were allowed to walk up the beach through the shoreline to cool our feet and legs and, on reaching the start, were sent off in small groups. I can remember telling Clive Walker, now with QPR, that there was no chance of me making the finish and so he invited me to run alongside him saying that he, too, was useless at any kind of distance running. I managed a mile but felt done for. It wasn't just a question of running gently along the beach either as there were rocks to be negotiated and beach-breaks to jump and I realised that I was even holding Clive back, but he and a couple of others insisted on staying with me and somehow talked me through to the end. Yet, despite the agony and the sheer pain I knew I liked the set-up and most of the other players, and wanted to sign for Chelsea. I think for their part the other players had warmed to me when they could see I was just a normal kind of fella who didn't fancy himself as some kind of superstar.

After the training I was told that the chairman wished to see me in his hotel in the early evening. The exertions of the morning had left us all shattered and after lunch some of us walked down into the town to visit the cinema for our afternoon off. Superman 3 was the film. What a joke, I was feeling more like Supergran! I don't remember much of the film anyway as I was haunted by the fear that I had blown my big chance of a transfer in the training session. Suppose they didn't think I was good enough, I asked myself, what then?

Again, I was impressed by the chairman's attitude when we came face to face once more. He made it quite clear the whole business had to be sorted out as quickly as possible. Sheila Marson, the Chelsea club secretary, had arrived from London with the necessary transfer and registration forms. Her appearance at the interview shook me a little bit because I had promised my Dad, my agent Brian, and Maurice Evans that I would not sign for Chelsea before consulting them about the deal. I was willing to reach agreement on personal terms with a proviso that I would be given time to discuss the entire situation with my friends and advisors. I had received a telephone call from Brian earlier in the day informing me that other clubs had now declared a definite interest at the fee being sought by Reading. Sheffield Wednesday and Watford were heading the queue behind Chelsea and Bobby Gould, the manager of Dad's old club Coventry City, was flying back from their pre-season tour to talk to me after I had returned from the meeting with Chelsea.

I had a sneaking feeling that Mr Bates was very much aware of what was happening and knew that I didn't want to sign for

Chelsea in Aberystwyth, even if I was willing to put pen to paper a little later. He made an extremely fair offer and was making it quite clear he had no intention of allowing me to leave Wales without having signed for Chelsea first. He warned me strongly that if I left Aberystwyth and talked to the other interested clubs, there was a strong possibility the Chelsea offer would be withdrawn. I was in a quandary, and did not know what to do for the best. Mr Bates sensed my indecision and left me alone in his hotel bedroom to think things over.

When he returned the powers of persuasion were switched on again. Time and again he impressed upon me that Chelsea was the right club for me and if I signed immediately I could undergo the necessary medical examination the following day and play for my new club on the Saturday. Everything about Chelsea appealed to me: I liked the chairman and manager; the players were my kind of people; but most of all there was a sense of ambition about them all. I knew that if I signed I would be part of a team which would shock a few people the following season and perhaps even make a dramatic return to the First Division. I'd made up my mind. I still insisted on talking to my Dad first and when the chairman asked me why I wanted to do this I had to tell him I consulted my parents about everything. He invited me to use his telephone to speak to whoever I wanted: 'Speak to who the hell you like, use my telephone, charge the calls to my account but at the end of it all I want you to sign.'

I told my Dad everything seemed okay and that I was going to sign for Chelsea immediately. He asked if I was under pressure and, although Mr Bates was sat on the other end of the bed and Sheila Marson was waiting patiently at the writing desk with the necessary forms neatly laid out, I managed to persuade him that all was well and there was no real pressure involved. I was going to sign for Chelsea whether in Aberystwyth or in London and at the end of the day it didn't matter either way. The chairman had done a great job as far as Chelsea was concerned. I could have insisted on returning home without signing and I am sure Mr Bates would have respected my wishes, but being the shrewd operator he was, and is, he didn't want the opposition to get near me. If I had been chairman of Chelsea I would have conducted the situation in exactly the same way and, if anything, he had risen even higher in my estimation. He wanted me and wasn't afraid to show it and, although he could have been bluffing when he warned the offer might be withdrawn if I didn't sign immediately, I wasn't prepared to take the chance. Men like Mr Bates are not to be trifled with.

As soon as I had put down the telephone I strode across to the desk where Sheila was waiting and signed the forms. I shook hands with Mr Bates. 'Welcome to Chelsea' he said. 'You won't regret the decision.' I wasn't too sure about that the following morning when I returned to London. I had been brought to Aberystwyth as a Reading player in the sumptuous luxury of the chairman's car. I returned as a Chelsea player in another vehicle with Sheila Marson at the wheel. It was a Mini. Mind you, I was pleased to be getting away from Aberystwyth and the killing training; I'd have sneaked a lift in a dustcart if necessary. All that lay ahead now was the medical examination at Charing Cross Hospital. I was a bit concerned about the pelvic injury of the previous season as if it showed up to be worse than I thought then the whole deal might be in jeopardy.

Dr Millington, Chelsea's club physician, was there to greet me and after checking on my general condition he asked if I had sustained any serious injuries in my career. I felt honour-bound to mention the pelvic injury and he conducted the normal X-rays to check if the problem was still apparent. He left the room for a considerable length of time and I began to fret there might be something seriously wrong. When he returned Dr Millington admitted the X-rays had revealed the pelvic condition was still there. I don't think I have ever felt so low as I did in that awful moment. I had visions of the deal collapsing with me returning to Reading to play in the Fourth Division because I was medically unfit. The doctor assured me I was, in general, a fit and healthy young athlete and asked if I was still experiencing pain from the pelvic area. I assured him there was no physical discomfort whatsoever. He left the room again, this time to telephone Mr Bates in Aberystwyth. In no time at all he was back to announce that the chairman and management at Chelsea were perfectly happy with my state of fitness after what they had seen for themselves in the training session. That god damned sand dune had come up trumps after all. I was happy but remained apprehensive although it was Chelsea's decision and they were paying the money. Happily, I think they are more than pleased with their investment.

I returned to Reading the following day as a fully-fledged Chelsea player. The lads were out training but I was able to have a long conversation with the new chairman Roger Smee. I thanked Maurice Evans for all he had done for me and waited for my old teammates to finish their training before bidding goodbye to them all. There was absolutely no doubt in my mind that signing for Chelsea presented a great opportunity to further my career. I'd come a long way from the emptiness of rejection by Luton and Tottenham in my early years and now my thoughts were of a strong push towards possible international honours, although I kept such notions strictly to myself. There was only one place to prove my worth – out on the field of play. I believed strongly that Chelsea remained one of the top clubs in the country despite their current Second Division status. Their determination to bring to an end the bad days was obvious to those privileged to witness Mr Bates at work. Money had been invested in new, ambitious players and the acumen of the management and coaching staff was first class. Chelsea were going places and I was going with them.

It didn't take long for me to discover the new signings plus one or two of the old guard at Chelsea were every bit as keen and ambitious as I was. John Neal had exploited the transfer market in the shrewdest possible way. He and his assistant Ian McNeill worked closely together and clearly had an instinct for young, unknown players with the ability to become household names. McNeill had an expert knowlege of the Scottish market which has provided a seemingly endless supply of superb football talent over many, many years. Some English managers had begun to suspect the golden goose was dying, but John and Ian knew differently. They had paid £90,000 to Morton for a big, gangling centre half called Joe McLaughlin which was hardly headline news, but Big Joe had the talent, desire and application to succeed. In my opinion he has matured into one of the finest central defenders in Britain who should have been a certainty in the Scotland World Cup squad. Little Pat Nevin has been saluted as some kind of genius reminiscent of Hughie Gallagher or Jimmy Johnstone. When he arrived at Chelsea as an £80,000 signing from Clyde he looked more like a waif and stray but the boy is a natural football artist, the kind the crowd willingly pay money to come and watch and he has been a revelation in English league football.

Ian McNeill has told me many times that he watched me play for Reading on umpteen occasions and was not too impressed. Then I would produce something in the opposition penalty area which made him sit up and promise himself to have another look. John Neal chipped in and in one newspaper article admitted: 'Everybody had heard about Dixon but not many would have touched him if they had seen the lad on the night when I went to watch him. Reading lost 1-0 at Gillingham and the lad missed three or four sitters. But I knew he would do for me.'

The fact that Neal and McNeill were able to achieve the miracle of Stamford Bridge is testimony to the cussedness of the chairman who worked out a policy with the management of pursuing players with both the ability and the will to succeed. Most players in the Third and Fourth Division would jump at the opportunity of joining a club like Chelsea. Many, however, would sadly not possess the necessary quality to harness to their enthusiasm.

John Hollins, as player-coach, was a vital acquisition from Arsenal and a major part of the new look Chelsea. He could still play a bit and possessed the drive and ambition of a sixteen-year-old. The new boys were integrated with the likes of David Speedie, John Bumstead, Colin Pates and Colin Lee; all honest professionals with a desire to succeed. From the first day I walked through the giant gates at Stamford Bridge it was obvious which players would soon be playing no further part in the future of the club. As much as the coaching staff attempted to keep everyone involved, the training sessions and the team formation in practice matches and pre-season friendlies betrayed the fact that many would soon be sold. As the season approached it became apparent that the resentment harboured by some of the old guard at Chelsea for the new players who had been brought in was going to cause problems. The dressing room banter was fearsome at times.

In the sixties, Chelsea had been one of most fashionable clubs in the country with a glamorous image provided by the likes of Peter Osgood, Charlie Cooke and Alan Hudson. It seemed to me that Hudson and the giant Mickey Droy, who had both been with the club in the great days, were the leaders of the faction which caused so much ill-feeling in the dressing room. Hudson insisted on doing his own thing and playing in his own way. He certainly didn't see eye to eye with the manager, coaching staff, or the new contingent of six players brought in to try and transform the fortunes of the club. When playing he wanted to pick the ball up off the central defenders and pass it out to the full back and was only interested in playing in a deep position. The management were adamant that he should play much further forward, just behind the front two in fact, where his extraordinary ability could be utilised in feeding the strikers and wingers. Hudson's stubbornness and sheer bloody-mindedness ensured he could not get into the team, which was a tragedy, but then much of his career could be described in similar terms. Here was a player blessed with the kind of ability mere mortals like myself could only dream about, and yet his attitude to the game in general and any kind of authority in particular blighted a talent which could so easily have been saluted as world class. Even when Hudson was finally squeezed out at Stamford Bridge his sniping continued with distasteful newspaper articles which slagged off the players he'd left behind at Chelsea. Perhaps he needed the money badly. I was one of his targets. He stated publicly that in his opinion I couldn't play and although there are some people in the game who would have upset me deeply if they'd come out with a similar appraisal of me, Hudson's words and opinions had long since ceased to count for anything.

The behaviour of Hudson and Droy threatened to destroy any semblance of team spirit at Chelsea. Neither was picked to play by John Neal in the team that was being hailed as 'the new Chelsea'. The two of them would watch the first half of matches at Stamford Bridge and if events on the pitch were not going particularly well they'd disappear into the player's bar for the rest of the game to pass derogatory comments on the men who had taken their places. Their behaviour made it easy for John Neal to reconcile himself with his decision that both must be moved out of Chelsea as quickly as possible.

Frankly, there were times when relationships were so strained between the new signings and the old guard that I was thankful I wasn't the only player who had been signed. At least there were six of us to take the flak. If I'd been on my own I reckon it could have proved impossible for me to remain at Chelsea. David Speedie, who had been signed by Chelsea from Darlington some time earlier, told me it had been a nightmare time for him. He couldn't seem to do anything right for them and he had almost reached desperation point. Fortunately, Speedo, as he is known by the lads, is made of sterner stuff. He was helped by a quiet word from John Neal who assured him the situation would change rapidly. The manager knew the chairman was prepared to back him to the hilt. John Neal and Speedo would stay, along with a handful of other decent lads and honest professionals, while the rest would be sold off. Speedo and I both discovered that John Neal is a man who lives up to his promises.

Mr Bates never seemed to be out of the news. He was forever among the headlines but the players saw very little of him in my initial time at Chelsea. There were a couple of occasions when he came in the dressing room and laid down the law as he saw it. He demanded strong discipline and high standards. We were told this was going to be the new era of Chelsea Football Club and any player, whether he had just signed or been there years, would be thrown out if he didn't pull his weight in the common cause.

A new back-bone to the team had been acquired: Eddie Niedzwiecki in goal, Joe McLaughlin at centre back and me at centre forward. Great professionals like Colin Pates, John Bumstead, Colin Lee, David Speedie, Joey Jones and Tony McAndrew were suplemented by Nigel Spackman, Pat Nevin and John Hollins. Surprisingly, Speedo, with whom I was later to form such an effective striking partnership, played below standard in the pre-season games of 1983-84 and was left out of the opening games, while I partnered Colin Lee at the front.

My own pre-season form wasn't much to write home about either. I scored my first goal for the club in a friendly at Wimbledon but we were beaten 2-1. However, I had begun to enjoy the strenuous training programme and was so keen to impress and do well, wanting to make an immediate impact. After the comparative serenity of Reading it really was all go at a club like Chelsea. The club was forever featured in the pages of all the national newspapers and when a press day was held at Stamford Bridge it seemed like every photographer in Britain wanted to take a picture.

I received an ideal confidence-booster just before the season started when I won the Shoot/Adidas Golden Shoe award for being the leading scorer in the Third Division with Reading the previous season. I'd scored twenty-six League goals in just thirty-five games which had made it a creditable total of fifty-one goals in 116 games for Reading since joining from non-league Dunstable.

The new season was almost upon us. I was, I admit, tentative and nervous about what might lie ahead. I'd scored goals all my life but I was going to need that ability now more than ever before and I had found it a strain to get used to new players with fresh ideas and different habits. At Reading I'd been allowed to settle down much more gently because in the opening year I'd been a part-time professional training on just two mornings a week with my new colleagues. It was early to bed for me on the night of

Friday, 26th August, 1983. The biggest test I had ever faced as a professional footballer was upon me. My debut for Chelsea the following day would be against Derby County who, under the management of Peter Taylor, were strong favourites for promotion. Instant hero or expensive flop? I was about to find out. There was no going back now.

7

GOALS, GOALS, GOALS

I could not have asked for a more memorable debut. The 'new Chelsea' were magnificent. The 5-0 trouncing of Derby County was the biggest win of the day in the entire Football League and Derby manager Peter Taylor, more famous as the right-hand man of Brian Clough at Nottingham Forest, confessed: 'We were humiliated and I don't like that, I'm not used to it.' I made one goal for Clive Walker and smacked in two of my own, the first a very satisfying half-volley. The Stamford Bridge crowd seemed to sense they might be in at the start of something good although we had not received a single mention as potential promotion candidates. Newcastle United, with the celebrated Kevin Keegan in their ranks, plus the super-fit Sheffield Wednesday and Manchester City were the outstanding favourites. No one in the Chelsea dressing room dared to mention that perhaps we would be in with a shout, but in our heart of hearts we had already begun to fancy the possibility.

The newspapers were full of our resounding success. 'Chelsea are top of the hit parade,' pronounced one headline. Another blazed: 'Kerry Gold'. I've been stuck with that one a few times since then! It appears to be the ready-made stand-by of sub-editors needing a label. Within a couple of days we had beaten Gillingham at their own Priestfield Stadium in the first leg of the Milk Cup first round. Gillingham scored first but, after I had managed to put Clive Walker through for the equaliser, I grabbed the winner with a header which gave me quite a bit of pleasure. We were on our way. It didn't take the newspapers long to latch on to a new name and immediately I was being compared to Peter Osgood, a great favourite of the past at Chelsea. I told them I'd never seen Osgood play, except on television, but I would settle for his achievements at Chelsea.

Two more goals in a 2-1 win at Brighton the following Saturday kept up the momentum. The supporters appeared to have taken an instant liking to my style of play and gave great encouragement to all of the new boys. A goalless draw at Blackburn followed by defeat at Sheffield Wednesday brought us back down to earth a bit, even though sandwiched in between was victory over a very poor Cambridge team and a 4-0 thrashing of Gillingham in the second leg of the Milk Cup. The Gillingham game was memorable for me because I was fortunate enough to score all of the goals, which made nine goals in my first six games for Chelsea. I could not have asked for anything more. Now I was being hailed as the new Malcolm Macdonald. Well at least that tag was a bit more accurate than the new Peter Osgood as Malcolm had been a particular favourite of mine. I had stood on the terraces at Luton when he was there and marvelled at his scintillating speed and deadly finishing.

The goals continued to flow, apart from one or two dry patches. Two against Huddersfield and Fulham and one which earned us a draw at Leeds on 26th November, 1983 put Chelsea second in the League. We were to surrender that position for just one game but a 6-1 thrashing of troubled Swansea, in which I scored one of the goals, re-established us as outstanding promotion material. In fact, we were not to fall away from the top two positions for the remainder of the season. But it was not sweetness and harmony all the way. Far from it. I didn't like David Speedie for a start.

The Dixon-Speedie striking combination has now grown to be one of the most feared in football. We are both extraordinarily competitive and the unrelenting desire to win is a fundamental part of our characters. Now we are good mates both on and off the field and I have a tremendous admiration for the fierce commitment, drive and outstanding energy of the little fellow. But it wasn't always like that I can tell you.

In my early days at Chelsea, Speedie was unable to claim a regular place in the team and instead his closest pal, Colin Lee, was selected to partner me at the front. David made it quite clear he believed he should be in the side and, probably because he was so close to Lee, I became the butt of his moans, groans and general displeasure, rather than suggesting to his mate that he shouldn't be in the team. Maybe I was over-sensitive, but I don't think that was the case, sensing a genuine animosity and definite jealousy in that I had been signed for a big fee and was grabbing the glory through the goals I had scored. Lee had played in the First Division with Spurs but I was just a country boy who had come up from the sticks at Dunstable and Reading. In fact, even when Speedie won a place in the team there was no let up in the situation. If I failed to control a ball in training he'd start giggling in a derisory manner, or raise his eyebrows in a kind of mock horror. Maybe it was because I was the new boy that I didn't bite back before I did, but a major confrontation was inevitable.

The situation exploded following a home game at Stamford Bridge on 3rd December, 1983 after we had been beaten by Manchester City, one of our great rivals for promotion. I'd been happy with my form recently: two goals from me and one from Paul Canoville had smashed Huddersfield's unbeaten home record of thirty-three matches; there had been another brace in the following Second Division game when we had beaten close rivals Fulham 5-3 at their own Craven Cottage ground; and a goal at Leeds gave us a 1-1 draw and pushed Chelsea into second position in the League for the first time that season. I had scored eleven goals in seventeen Second Division games plus the Milk Cup goals before our match with Manchester City. There was an expectant buzz at Stamford Bridge that day. City had been favourites to return to the First Division from the very start of the season and now Chelsea were much in contention. There was a crowd of 29,142 at the game but I was trying to concentrate on doing well for the team. I had already warned our centre half, Joe McLaughlin, who had become my closest pal, that if there were any more derogatory comments from Speedie I was going to hit him. He and Lee had been having a go at me throughout the previous week in training sessions and I knew that if I made even the slightest mistake they'd throw their hands up in exasperation and glare at me as though I was some kind of imbecile.

I have always believed that one of my great assets as a goalscorer is an uncanny sixth sense as to where the ball will drop in a crowded penalty area. It was from one of these attacking situations that the bad feeling between Speedie, Lee and myself came to a head. The team was not playing well and we were a goal behind after Jim Tolmie had scored for Manchester City. Speedie had started the game up front with me and Lee had been introduced from the substitute bench in place of Peter Rhoades-Brown, in order to provide a three-pronged attack. One of the players was about to cross the ball and Lee urged me to make a run towards the near post. I ignored him because I was expecting the ball to be played into the crowded goalmouth. In the event the centre was played towards the near post and the possible chance of an equaliser had gone because I had not made the run. Both Lee and Speedie immediately began their sniping criticisms. I snapped.

I warned Speedie that if he opened his mouth once more I'd put my fist in it. He looked shocked and muttered something like: 'Oh, you just do your own thing then.' There were about five minutes remaining in the match and my anger was raging. As soon as we returned to the dressing room I challenged Speedie: 'Have you got anything else to say?' I demanded. 'Oh, shut up,' came the reply. I saw red and punched him in the face. He tried to retaliate but other players rushed in between the two of us and kept us apart. 'Right,' I stormed, 'we'll finish this later.' No serious damage had been done but manager John Neal was not at all amused by the episode and ordered the pair of us to report to his office as soon as we had changed out of our playing kit.

I felt empty and hollow inside. The weeks of pent-up emotion were now out in the open. My temper had not subsided by the time I was in the manager's office where I told John Neal that I was not prepared to endure the situation a moment longer, while he sat behind his desk quietly contemplating my rage. I told him there would be a written transfer request on his desk by the Monday morning and made it clear I was no longer prepared to play in the same team as Speedie. There was no way I was willing to stay with a club where I was being slaughtered by teammates intent on taking the mickey at every available opportunity. 'I'm finished with this club, I want away,' I concluded. For once Speedie had remained quiet. Finally he spoke: 'People can't say anything to you but it's okay for you to do it.' I retorted that ever since I had joined Chelsea in the summer he had made my life a misery when it should have been one of joy after the goals I had scored. Speedie was silent. I looked at him and much of the anger drained away. It's impossible to explain but I began to feel sorry for him, not in a demeaning way, but as though I had been enlightened by a spark of understanding of his motives. Perhaps his own great desire to be a success as a professional footballer had overwhelmed him. He looked genuinely upset and disturbed by what had happened between us and on reflection I had reacted in totally the wrong way. Even though Joe McLaughlin insisted later I had been right to strike him I knew I had been out of order. It was silly, emotional stuff and two responsible men should have known better.

John Neal brought the altercation to a close by ordering me to report to his office on the Monday morning, while Speedie was instructed to stay behind that night. I don't know to this day what was said to Speedie after I had left the ground. I returned home and related the story of the dramatic events to my Dad who told me to forget the idea of a transfer for the moment although he accepted the situation could not be allowed to continue. He advised me to let the manager sort things out and we would decide on our next move if John Neal was unable to do so. I was happy enough to forget about the transfer threat because it had been made in the heat of the moment. When I reported to the ground on the Monday morning, no one said anything to me about the incident and after saying good-morning to everyone I went out to do my training. I have never been the type of person to bear a grudge and thankfully the matter was closed.

It seemed that the clash between Speedie and myself was the best thing that could have happened as our relationship, both personally and professsionally, blossomed from that point onwards. Maybe the outburst allowed us both to understand the other's temperament much more than we had previously. He certainly seemed to realise I was every bit as competitive as himself and, for my part, I came to admire his gutsy, passionate approach to his profession. Of course, he's a moaner but certainly no more than I am. We have won an outstanding reputation as a partnership, still criticising each other but now the tone is different. We keep each other on our toes on and off the pitch and I have come to like Speedie the man very much indeed.

I'm not the only player who has come to blows with Speedie at one time or another but, in my opinion, all these fracas have been part of the fabric in weaving Chelsea into the fine team it is today. In those early days of the 'new Chelsea' the team consisted of players who were desperate to be a success as we were all aware this might prove to be the only chance we would be given. Speedie was no different from the rest. He'd been signed from Darlington and had no intention of going back into the lower divisions. These altercations were born out of pride and ambition and John Neal must have been secretly delighted by the reaction from the new team he had formed, expecially after the nightmares of the previous season. The spirit within the camp grew and grew until there was a warm feeling of complete togetherness throughout the squad. The moans and groans gave way to encouragement and collectiveness. We were determined to get out of the Second Division together. The six new players, backed by the likes of Speedie and Joey Jones who were tremendous competitors, plus the skills of Colin Pates and the determination of John Bumstead, made us an irresistable force.

Our confidence had been boosted by a Milk Cup second round

victory over First Division Leicester. We won 2-0 at their ground, were beaten 2-0 on our own pitch in the second leg, finally reaching the third round through a 4-3 victory in the penalty shoot-out. But hopes of Wembley were terminated in the next round when we went down 1-0 at home to West Brom. With that particular Cup diversion out of the way we were able to concentrate on our promotion ambitions. My fight with Speedie after the game against Manchester City could hardly have been said to have upset the team. In the next match we thrashed Swansea 6-1 at Stamford Bridge with Paul Canoville collecting a hat-trick and a goalless draw at Barnsley the following week provided the point which took us back into second position in the Second Division.

Sheffield Wednesday had been at the top of the table right from the start of the season and everybody expected them to stay there until the finish – except Chelsea. We were pressing them hard but then came a game which I took a long time to forget – against Portsmouth at Stamford Bridge on 27th December. Mark Hateley, now with AC Milan and my great rival for the number nine shirt in the England team, put Pompey ahead with a header after just three minutes. Paul Canoville equalised for us but, when I dropped back to help out the defence, I handled a centre from Nicky Morgan and Kevin Dillon restored Portsmouth's lead with the penalty. A couple of minutes later we had a penalty after Speedie had been brought down. I'd scored from the spot in each of the previous two matches so I had no qualms about taking this one. I hit it well enough but goalkeeper Alan Knight saved brilliantly. I managed to atone a little for that miss by scoring our equaliser with just seven minutes of the first half remaining. But there was even more drama to come. Speedie was brought down again and we had a second penalty which could win us the match and three precious points. I decided to change the direction in which I would hit the ball, beating the goalkeeper this time but striking the crossbar. The newspapers had a field day although John Neal insisted afterwards that if we were awarded another penalty in the match against Brighton four days later he would still want me to take it. I wasn't so sure. We struggled at Brighton on the last day of 1983 and, as usual, had a massive following of supporters away from home. With forty minutes of the match remaining we were awarded a penalty. I remember thinking: 'Oh no, not again.' Some of the lads wanted me to take it, others didn't but I decided I had to do it because if I chickened out the confidence of the whole team might be affected. Our supporters roared and cheered as I picked up the ball, which encouraged me, and I concentrated totally on striking the ball well. I achieved that all right but goalkeeper Joe Corrigan threw his massive bulk to his right and pulled off a truly magnificent save, while I just wanted a huge hole to open and swallow me up as a big groan went up from the fans. The fact that Speedie scored a winning goal for us with just eleven minutes remaining cheered me a little but I vowed there and then that I would never take another penalty. If the truth be told I think I resigned just before I was about to be sacked.

Speedie's goal, just one of many vital strikes that season from him, had taken Chelsea to the top of the Second Division for the first time. We were overjoyed about that, of course, but far from happy about the management decision to take us immediately to Middlesbrough for our next game on 2nd January. The normal proceedure would have been to travel to the north-east on the day before the game but, obviously, the management were concerned that the players might overdo the New Year celebrations. It's a long trip from Brighton to Middlesbrough and the club had promised there would be a hot meal waiting for us at the hotel. The discontent of the players was increased when we discovered all there was on offer were a couple of plates of sandwiches and a few sad looking lettuce leaves. It was an incongruous situtation. There we were a team on top of the Second Division walking around with faces like wet weeks. Thankfully John Hollins took charge of the situation and in agreement with the manager decided we should go out to a restaurant for a hot meal. The news cheered the players considerably and when we returned from the restaurant at about 11.00pm John Neal informed us we could also see the New Year in, as long as we were in our beds shortly after midnight. Some of the lads didn't think that was a particularly good idea as the match wasn't until 2nd January. Having had a few drinks we were in no mood to go to bed while the New Year festivities were held in our absence. Sure enough, shortly after midnight, the manager was ushering us up to our rooms. We pleaded for more time and a few of us tried to hide from him while John was getting more and more annoyed. A few of the lads were a bit tipsy and understandably the manager didn't like it one bit. By 1.00am all of the players were in their beds and sleeping soundly but there was to be no escaping the rollicking which awaited us the next morning. I don't think I had ever seen the manager so annoyed. The lecture made us all the more determined to do well for him at Middlesbrough the following day.

Alas, it didn't work out that way. I missed an open goal almost at the start and many of the lads produced performances which were well below par. We were a goal down at half-time but Tony McAndrew, a player who had been with Middlesbrough when John Neal was manager there, scored an equaliser. It was a filthy, horrible day, it rained incessantly and the pitch was an absolute quagmire. Our goalkeeper, Eddie Niedzwiecki, slipped unfortunately as he was drop-kicking the ball out of his hands allowing it to slither to the edge of the penalty area where one of their strikers, David Currie, reacted to the situation before our defenders and went around Eddie scoring easily. There was a deathly silence in our dressing room after that game. The players were convinced the celebrations of New Year's Eve had nothing to do with our lacklustre performance but it was immediately evident the management did not concur with our viewpoint. John Neal was fuming while his assistant Ian McNeill was speechless. John Hollins had a real go at the players.

It was a long trip back to London. The players were dejected because we knew in our heart of hearts that teams like Middlesbrough should have provided no obstacle if we were to win promotion at the end of the season. We were back in second position and matters were hardly improved by a 1-0 defeat in the third round of the FA Cup at Blackburn Rovers. The manager made it clear to us all he was not prepared to stand by and risk the distinct possibility of Chelsea squandering an outstanding opportunity to return to the First Division. His solution was to buy the Welsh international Mickey Thomas – an inspired move. John Neal knew all about Thomas' potential because he had brought him into the game when he was manager at Wrexham. Thomas proved not only good for the club because of his football talent but also for his extrovert personality. He, along with his Welsh teammate Joey Jones, had an impish sense of humour and they were great for team spirit, lifting everybody's morale.

A 2-1 win at Derby County – with Tony McAndrew hitting the winner from a penalty – set us up for the highlight of the season so far: a home match against our great rivals Sheffield Wednesday on 21st January. In front of 35,147 spectators Chelsea stormed into a two goal lead before half-time, Mickey Thomas scoring both of them, and a third from Pat Nevin ensured that the two Wednesday scored, through Mark Smith and Gary Banister, would not be enough to prevent us going back to the top of the Second Division. Two more goals from me and a contribution from Speedie saw off Huddersfield in the next match and then Cambridge were beaten by a Tony McAndrew goal. The pressure at the top was intense and the fact we only managed a draw at home to Carlisle was enough to put Wednesday back above us. On 3rd March another penalty from McAndrew, plus goals from Speedie and myself in a 3-0 defeat of Oldham Athletic, enabled us to sneak above Wednesday once more, followed by a draw at Newcastle against Kevin Keegan's team, and a 2-1 home win over Blackburn Rovers maintained our position. The team was playing with terrific confidence and not even the shock of falling three goals behind in a game at Cardiff could knock us out of our stride. Second-half goals from myself, Colin Lee and a penalty, this time from Nigel Spackman, earned us a point. I managed two more on target in the 4-0 thrashing of local rivals Fulham but ironically we lost our top spot to Sheffield Wednesday once more on goal difference.

The first priority of us all was to clinch promotion and yet none of us would have been completely satisfied if we did not make a determined bid to win the Second Division Championship itself.

And so it was that on a warm, sunny afternoon Leeds United came to Stamford Bridge. Memories of Saturday 7th April, 1984 will not be easily erased, as we were all aware that victory would ensure First Division football for Chelsea. I scored two goals in the first half and another eight minutes after the interval, while Mickey Thomas had put us on our way with a goal in only the fifth minute. The Chelsea supporters among a crowd of 33,447 were eager to celebrate and five minutes before the end many of them had left the terraces and were only yards away from the pitch, where they were held back by a ring of policemen. A minute from full-time Paul Canoville, who had come on as substitute, scored a glorious fifth goal and the crowd went wild pouring onto the pitch.

The referee, Gilbert Napthine of Sileby in Leicestershire, was knocked over in the rush, and the worry was that the match would not be allowed to finish. But Mr Napthine recovered after treatment and insisted the incident had been a pure accident, understanding fully the excitement and exuberance of our supporters who, fortunately, responded to an appeal over the loudspeaker system to vacate the playing area. However, it was obvious that the moment the final whistle was sounded the players would be mobbed. Mr Napthine, very much aware of the problem, awarded a free kick and then whispered to the players to pass the word round that he was about to end the game. Most of us edged towards the players' entrance and when the referee sounded the final whistle managed to escape unscathed. It was a very intelligent move and I have no hesitation in applauding Mr Napthine for being responsible for the most sensible piece of refereeing I have experienced in my entire career.

So Chelsea were promoted and how the supporters celebrated. Mr Napthine's action had ensured the players were able to celebrate with them in the correct manner in the director's box where we were saluted by our supporters who were by now massed on the pitch. Although I was overjoyed for everyone connected with the club my own mood of sheer elation was still tempered by a feeling of sadness for Leeds United. They, too, had enjoyed some great days in their past. Chelsea were back in the First Division but it seemed to me that Leeds had some way to go before they could anticipate a similar celebration. Hopes had been high among their supporters that they too could win promotion but our 5-0 victory had pushed them down to twelfth position and the result coupled with the unbridled joy of our supporters made it too much to bear for some of their fans. Our electric scoreboard was smashed and pieces of bricks and masonry struck some of the policemen on duty; an unsavoury scene for a few brief moments, which was quickly and effectively subdued by police.

We were now all doubly determined to win the Championship. Our next match against Manchester City, whose own promotion challenge had sadly faded, was to be televised live. The talk was of the new young, vibrant team about to tackle the First Division and, as ever, there was a large contingent from Chelsea among the crowd. With their encouragement we produced an impressive performance for the television cameras. My goal was the epitome of the splendid team play which had become our hallmark in the second half of the season. Paul Canoville combined with David Speedie, and I headed the cross into the net. The quality of the goal was recognised by the fact it became one of the contenders for the title of 'Goal of the Season'. Pat Nevin provided the second in a comprehensive victory.

A home win over Barnsley set it all up for a Championship decider in the last match of the season. With Sheffield Wednesday being held to a goalless draw at home by Manchester City we were back on top, having edged ahead on goal difference, so we knew that victory at Grimsby would guarantee us the Second Division Championship. My roommate on away trips, Joe McLaughlin, and I had speculated for some time about the possibility of having to win at Grimsby in order to take the title. Blundell Park is not the most hospitable ground to visit in search of a crucial result and Grimsby had enjoyed a good season themselves, Portsmouth being the only team who had been able to win on their ground previously. Sheffield Wednesday's task, a visit to struggling Cardiff City, appeared much the easier to us, but our determination to succeed would, we believed, be a telling factor.

There were 13,000 people crammed into Blundell Park, their second highest attendance of the entire season, and most of them appeared to be Chelsea fans. The section of the ground allocated to Chelsea supporters just couldn't contain the sheer weight of numbers and with just a quarter of an hour of the game gone many spectators spilled over the barriers gasping for air. The referee took the players off the field and back to the dressing rooms until the supporters had been housed comfortably. The game was suspended for a full fifteen minutes which meant the vital match at Ninian Park would finish before our game.

I had a chance to ease our nerves and put us in front, although my first shot had rebounded to safety off the legs of the Grimsby goalkeeper Nigel Batch. He denied me again a little later but five minutes before half-time I left him helpless. Pat Nevin had gone past a couple of defenders out on the right before crossing perfectly and I met the ball full on the forehead putting us ahead. However, the drama was far from over. Grimsby attacked furiously and our goal mouth enjoyed a charmed life, although we were still dangerous in breakaways and Joe McLaughlin had a header cleared off the line. Suddenly, we were awarded a penalty when Speedie was brought down. I certainly wasn't looking to take it and Pat Nevin stepped forward. He was under incredible pressure because he knew a goal for Chelsea at that stage would confirm us as champions. He hit his shot to the goalkeeper's right but Batch produced a great save. The pressure increased when the news came though that Sheffield Wednesday had won 2-0 at Cardiff. We were now forced to defend furiously. Joe McLaughlin was brilliant at holding us together, playing better than ever. When the final whistle sounded the first emotion was of incredible relief and then a feeling of tremendous euphoria. We all celebrated with a few beers on the trip back to London, understandably satisfied with our performance. Chelsea had won promotion before, of course, but they had never returned to the First Division as champions.

For the moment I was happy enough to reflect on a fantastic first season for myself. I'd scored a total of thirty-four goals which was the best in the division, a total of twenty-eight in the League and six in the Milk Cup and it could have been more had I not missed those three penalties. But perhaps most pertinent of all was the fact we had not lost a single League game since that fateful day of 2nd January when we had been shamed at Middlesbrough. We'd won thirteen of the last seventeen games and drawn the other four. The 1983-84 football season had indeed provided the most exciting and eventful part of my career up until that time.

FIRST DIVISION AT LAST

Our celebrations soon turned to feelings of great shock and sadness when we learned that John Neal had almost died in taking Chelsea Football Club back into the First Division. The mood had been so bouyant, so light-hearted and even chairman Ken Bates had joined in the festivity.

After thrashing Leeds, which meant promotion was a certainty, the players had secretly planned to throw Mr Bates in the team bath. He must have got wind of what was going on because he strolled into the dressing room, calm as you please, and said: 'Okay boys, I'll go quietly.' With that he jumped fully clothed into the bath and sat there among the boys with his suit saturated and the water dripping off his spectacles. The incident illustrates perfectly the kind of bloke Mr Bates has proved to be. He's a good sport and a lot more human than the media would have you believe. Mind you, I suspect he enjoys his public image. To me he is not so much an ogre as a mischievious rascal! Anyone who spends time with a football team has to be prepared for a deal of mickey-taking and hc stands up to it well, getting his own back with the most awful jokes imaginable which he insists on telling us before a game. No wonder all of the players cannot wait to get out of the dressing room and onto the pitch! From my observations, the chairman doesn't interfere with the football management side of things at all, leaving the staff to run the team while he takes charge of all business matters. He seems to have done a marvellous job with a club which was on the brink of bankruptcy when he took command. Of course, I have known only the new Chelsea. The lads who were part of the club during the previous regime must have found the transformation much more dramatic and the new signings had obviously made a hell of a difference. The players already at the club realised quickly that the new boys were ambitious and possessed a tremendous desire to be successful.

John Neal had clearly done a fantastic job in rejuvenating Chelsea and was a nice man who commanded great respect from all of the players. So it came as a bombshell to us all when we were informed he had undergone emergency open-heart surgery in the summer of 1984. We had suspected for some time that his health was not as sound at it might have been, as there were times towards the end of the previous season when he had to abandon the trainer's bench in the later stages of vital matches. I think we all thought the pressure might be getting to him but little did we know that he was a very sick man indeed. So often the newspapers employ exaggerated adjectives to highlight the dramas of football, describing many players as great when in fact they are merely good and carrying quotes from players who talk of dying for their club in important matches. On this occasion there was no need for journalistic licence; John Neal had almost killed himself with the effort of restoring Chelsea's First Division heritage.

When the full facts emerged we learnt that John had undergone a life and death operation involving four separate by-passes and lasting five hours in London's Princess Grace hospital. It seemed he had no alternative but to agree to the major surgery because he had been told in no uncertain terms that the arteries around his heart were ninety-five per cent useless. A massive heart-attack was imminent. He had been suffering discomfort for some time but it was only before our last match of the season, at Grimsby where we needed to win to take the Championship, that other people observed just how ill he was. In fact he had been unable to withstand the final fifteen minutes at Blundell Park and had returned to the dressing room.

It is ironic that the man who had been forced to employ major surgery of his own to prevent Chelsea Football Club from dying was himself placed at the mercy of skilful surgeons who were to save his own life. It is at those times that the value of football is put into its true perspective. The legendary Bill Shankly was once quoted as saying: 'Football is not a matter of life and death – it's more important than that.' John Neal's passion for the game ran as deep as anyone I know but I doubt if he agreed with Shanks as he lay in that hospital bed.

John had a great passion for his cigarettes and never seemed to have one out of his mouth. They obviously provided him with great comfort when the pressure was on but it was made clear to him by the doctors that they had to go. I understand he insisted on one last fag before the operation and he's not touched one since, thank goodness. I sent him a get-well card but I'm sure it would have been just one of thousands. John Neal was, and is, of course, a very popular, highly-respected man. It was fascinating to read an interview with him when he was well on the way to recovery. He talked of the job he had been able to do at Chelsea and thanked the chairman for providing him with the opportunity when all around believed he would be sacked: 'The players I got rid of were nice enough lads,' he said. 'But some of them were not very good professionals. I am very satisfied with the value I have got from the money I spent on new signings. We also got some excellent money for some very ordinary players when it came to selling a few. The lads we have bought must have increased considerably in value because when they came to Chelsea they were comparatively unknown.'

I was particularly interested in his comments on my signing from Reading. He observed: 'Everybody had heard of Dixon but not many would have touched him if they had seen the lad on the night when I went to watch him. Reading lost 1-0 at Gillingham and Dixon missed three sitters. But I knew he would do for me. At the outset Reading were talking ridiculous prices so I switched my attention to Mark Hateley who was playing for Coventry City at that time. But I couldn't match what Portsmouth were willing to pay the lad. But it's amazing how lucky you can be. Dixon became available at a sensible fee and I signed him. It has always been my opinion he is a better centre forward than Hateley. We'll find out if he's good enough to play for England when Bobby Robson picks him – and that's inevitable. Then I'll settle down in my seat and allow myself a little chuckle when he bangs in the goals. Mark my words he won't let me down.' I have to admit that seeing John's words in print filled me with pride. I hadn't dared to think I could possibly play for England . . . well not openly anyway. My main task was to establish myself as a recognised goalscorer in the First Division, and that was not going to be easy as I was soon to discover.

It all started well enough for both Chelsea and me. The opening game was a London derby match against Arsenal at Highbury. It was the club's first game in the top flight after seven years in the Second Division, the date was 25th August, 1984 and there was a crowd of 45,329 inside the ground on a warm, sunny morning. I was feeling fit and excited at my own personal debut in the First Division. The pre-season work, dreaded by most professional footballers, had gone well and not even the terror of another visit to Aberystwyth for the relentless grind up and down the sand dunes had seemed as bad as previously. I'd tried to stay in reasonable shape during the close season playing a lot of squash and badminton with my mates in Luton. Most professionals these days attempt to ease the dread of pre-season training by doing a bit themselves before they report back to their clubs after the summer break. I suppose some of us believe it will give us a head start on the other lads but it never seems to work out that way.

I think all of the Chelsea players were a little bit nervous when we stepped out at Highbury for the morning kick-off, even though the private ambition within the dressing room was to finish high enough in the First Division to qualify for European combat. There were certainly no thoughts or fears that we might be relegated. We knew we had the makings of an outstanding football team and were determined to fulfill that potential. The welcome we received from the Chelsea fans was incredible. We had become conditioned to their massive support away from home without ever taking it for granted. There must have been 20,000 of them in that Highbury ground and we were so grateful to see them all again wanting us to give them something to cheer about. During the close season the club had signed a big, rugged Scotsman called Doug Rougvie. None of us knew what to expect from the full-back who had been transferred from Aberdeen for £180,000, but we were soon to find out. Arsenal's England right back, Viv Anderson, made a run down the right and made the mistake of overruning the ball slightly. That was enough for our new man. He went into the tackle so hard that Viv went about six feet up in the air and catapulted over the top of Doug. Our man then went striding away with the ball and our supporters went wild with delight. I remember thinking: 'Good grief, what have we got here?' He was like a tank. Doug was to become the butt of many a dressing room joke but he took them all in good heart. A super fellow is Doug Rougvie.

We had started the game brightly enough but Paul Mariner headed Arsenal in front after thirty-five minutes from a free kick by Kenny Sansom. Just four minutes later came one of the most exciting moments of my entire life – my first ever goal in the First Division. Doug Rougvie put over a free kick and I latched on to the ball as it bounced in the Arsenal penalty area. I hit it first time with my left foot but the shot rebounded off the legs of Pat Jennings and looped into the air. I was able to react a split-second faster than the Arsenal defenders and volleyed home the rebound with my right foot. At last I had emulated my Dad and scored a goal in Division One. That had always been his claim to fame and now I had achieved it as well. A draw was probably a fair result. We were suitably pleased with ourselves because Arsenal were one of the clubs strongly fancied to do well in the coming season. A 1-0 win over Sunderland in our first home game two days later, with another timely goal from Paul Canoville, provided a satisfactory beginning.

The next game was scheduled for the Friday night because it was to be televised live. Our chairman, Mr Bates, was totally against whole matches being transmitted by television, convinced that live coverage would kill football. However, the players were quite excited about it as the cameras provided a bit more spice to the occasion and we had played magnificently at Manchester City in our previous presentation before the nation. Unfortunately, the game against Everton hardly lived up to its billing and turned out to be probably one of the most disappointing games seen on television to date.

Everton had completed the last season in terrific style, capturing the FA Cup by beating Watford at Wembley. Their manager, Howard Kendall, had clearly turned the club around because they had previously been in the doldrums for a long time. Much was expected of them in that 1984-85 season but, surprisingly, they had not begun at all well. A 4-1 home defeat by Tottenham on the opening day of the season had been followed by a 2-1 deficit at West Brom. Chelsea and Everton were as bad as each other that night. I hit the crossbar on one occasion and missed a couple of half-chances. Everton seemed perfectly happy to go home with their first point of the season with a draw when, out of the blue, they grabbed a surprise winner with a shot from Kevin Richardson under our goalkeeper Eddie Niedzwiecki. The Chelsea lads were really down after that. It was our first defeat in the First Division and our performance in front of millions of spectators had been well below par. In fact, it was our first League defeat since 2nd January at Middlesbrough. We consoled ourselves with the knowledge we had been no worse than Everton despite the defeat. Little did we know then that Everton would march to the top of the First Division early in November. Later we were to force them away from the summit for a time but they climbed back in January and stayed there to complete a marvellous season. They took the League Championship and the European Cup Winners Cup, but failed to pull off an incredible treble success being beaten by Manchester United in extra time of the FA Cup Final.

The prospect of a visit to Manchester United in the next match was daunting to say the least. The crowd of 48,398 at Old

Trafford was the biggest I had ever played in front of and in the opening twenty minutes United produced the best football I have ever seen. If Eddie Niedzwiecki had not been in such superlative form they would have been five goals clear before we'd earned so much as a kick. Jesper Olsen scored for United but we battled back marvellously and Mickey Thomas was just a little bit chuffed to provide the well earned equaliser against one of his old clubs. I was pleased for Mickey but becoming increasingly concerned at my own form. I hadn't made the impact I had so desperately craved in First Division football and the situation went from bad to worse in the next game. I hadn't scored since the opening game of the season against Arsenal and was extremely anxious about the situation. I was snapping at goalscoring chances instead of putting them away in my usual fashion, despite having learned in my early days as a professional at Reading that it is essential for a striker to take his time in front of goal. If he snatches at chances, the odds are he'll blaze them over the crossbar or wide of the posts. I was playing like a novice and I knew it. I'd had to live with inevitable speculation about whether I possessed the skills and temperament to be a success at the highest level. It had never bothered me previously and I was confident enough in my own ability. After all, I'd been on trial from the moment I signed as a professional with Reading and had still managed to produce goals in the Third Division and become top scorer in the Second Division with Chelsea. The newspapers clearly believed my discomfort made for compulsive reading as their columns were flooded with repeated analysis of what they termed 'the Dixon dilemma'. I'd even begun to believe they might be right; maybe I couldn't score goals in the First Division; maybe I had found the true pinnacle of my potential in the Second Division.

While John Neal was recouperating from his operation, assistant-manager Ian McNeill and player-coach John Hollins were in charge, although none of the players ever knew which one of them was actually picking the team. Despite my depressed state, I was still chosen to play in our next game against Aston Villa. It was a day I'd rather forget. We were comprehensively beaten 4-2 by Aston

Villa and for the first time in my career at Chelsea I was pulled off. I knew I wasn't playing well but was devastated when I saw the card carrying the number nine held up on the touchline. I went down to the dressing room and sat alone in the team bath. I was desolate, oblivious to the roar of the crowd as the game went on without me. I was at the crossroads in my career and I knew it. I'd set my own standards as a goalscorer and I had failed woefully to live up to them. I reported for training again the following week, determined to snap out of my slump. I was in for another surprise which brought the entire situation to a head.

Derek Johnstone, who had played for Scotland in the 1978 World Cup finals in Argentina, was the reserve centre forward at Stamford Bridge and had scored a couple of goals in a Football Combination game the previous night. Since the reserves had played a match I was surprised to see Johnstone report for training the following morning with the first team squad of thirteen players. All kinds of thoughts and fears flooded into my mind. I was convinced Johnstone had been instructed to report for training with a view to taking my place in the game at West Ham on the Saturday and I was equally sure that this was not the way to ease me out of my bad patch. My anger prevented me from concentrating on the training and immediately after the session I sought a meeting with Hollins and demanded to know what was going on. I told him in no uncertain terms that if I was about to be dropped then he'd better tell me to my face. He took the wind out of my sails a bit when he replied calmly: 'What gave you that idea?' Before I could say another word he went on: 'As far as I am concerned you stay in the team to play yourself out of the bad patch.' I was taken aback but not completely appeased, so Hollins went on to explain that Johnstone had volunteered to come in for extra training and that no one had requested him to do so.

I knew at once what Johnstone had been up to. He'd read the newspapers, he'd known I'd been pulled off at Villa the previous Saturday, and having scored a couple of goals himself in the reserve team was determined to stake his claim. He was putting the squeeze on me. That was the last thing I needed as I was depressed enough already. Now I was really down in the dumps. It was all getting too much for me to handle and now one of my own teammates was gunning for me. On reflection it was a silly attitude for me to take and I have to say now I cannot blame him in the slightest. He had his own ambitions and here was a chance for him to get in the team. There was nothing wrong in what he did, it was rather my own basic insecurity that had got the better of me. In fact, that was the only occasion, to my knowledge, that Johnstone reported for extra training. Hollins was as good as his word and I was named in the team which met West Ham at Stamford Bridge. I made a goal for David Speedie in a 3-0 win, in fact I'd played quite well, much better than in previous games, but I still hadn't scored. A goal was what I needed most of all. Hollins boosted my confidence a little by telling me he had been much more satsified with my contribution. But it was John Neal who soothed my nerve-ends most of all. He had looked in at the ground following his operation and he offered his usual sound advice, telling me not to worry and to concentrate on playing my normal game. The boss had always been a great believer in simplicity and he was adamant I should stick to what I did best to help the goals to flow again. He believed once I was back on target all my problems would be behind me, assuring me he was still the manager at Chelsea, even though his convalescence was not complete, and that I would always be in his team. Hollins and Neal had both been good to me in my hour of need. The situation had presented the greatest crisis of my career to date and they had provided much-needed comfort in expressing unequivocally their unswerving confidence in me.

Our next meeting with Luton Town, at Kenilworth Road, seemed to me to be the appropriate venue to end my bad patch, after my previous association with that club. My mates in the town supported Luton but they were acutely aware of my discomfort and would have been delighted if I'd scored a hat-trick. But it was not to be. In fact, nobody scored in a disappointing 0-0 draw and the newspapers were at it again: 'Dixon's head on the block,' screamed one headline. Suddenly, everything began to go right for me – the match a Milk Cup second round first leg tie at Stamford Bridge against Millwall. In the twenty-eighth minute I played a through ball for David Speedie, and the Millwall defender Mickey Nutton, once of Chelsea, diverted the ball past his own goalkeeper. Less than a minute later I was celebrating joyously my first goal in seven games, a beauty, even if I do say so myself. I received a pass from Doug Rougvie, went passed defender Dave Cusack, and shot across the goalkeeper into the far corner. It was as if a huge burden had been lifted off my shoulders. Six minutes into the second half I got my second goal of the game when a bad back pass from a Millwall defender let me in. My confidence was not fully restored because, although Millwall had presented formidable opposition, they were not a First Division club. In the event, they exacted revenge on Chelsea later in the season by beating us 3-2 at Stamford Bridge in the fourth round of the FA Cup, when I was forced to miss the game through injury, and eventually secured promotion from the Third Division.

After the game assistant-manager Ian McNeill told the press: 'They were very important goals indeed for Kerry Dixon. But he's got to keep going now because I thought he went back into his shell later in the game.' He may have been right but I could feel my confidence start to come back and and couldn't wait for the First Division game at home to Leicester on the Saturday. I got the first two goals in a 3-0 victory and although I failed to score in a goalless draw at Norwich the following week I knew inside myself that I was back in the groove.

However, two goals against Watford didn't prevent another home defeat, with John Barnes, later to become my roommate with England, providing a brilliant winner, and a 1-0 defeat at Southampton dumped Chelsea into fourteenth place in the First Division. But not for long. I got both the goals in a 2-0 win over Ipswich and was especially pleased because I was up against Terry Butcher, a player I rate extremely highly regarding my confrontation with him as a special challenge.

Coventry City were the next visitors to Stamford Bridge and I looked forward to the meeting eagerly because it was to be my first game against my Dad's old club. My confidence was sky high by this stage but the whole team was staggered by Coventry's opening which produced two goals from Mickey Gynn and Bob Latchford in the first twenty-seven minutes. I pulled one back with a header from a Paul Canoville corner on the half hour and was involved in a move which led to an equaliser from Keith Jones shortly before half-time. In the second half we ran amok; Coventry just couldn't hold us. In the sixty-ninth minute I sent Canoville away and his cross was swept in by David Speedie. Then a superb cross from Pat Nevin enabled me to head my second goal of the game. I was faintly surprised to see the electric scoreboard at Stamford Bridge light up with the message: 'Come on Kerry, you're not going home until you get your hat-trick.' Within ten minutes I'd been able to oblige – this time with a shot. Keith Jones got a sixth before the end and the Chelsea team was naturally jubilant.

The game had provided my first hat-trick in the First Division and amazingly, after such a sad, confusing start to the season, I was established as the leading scorer in the League with ten goals from thirteen games, which represented nine goals in the last six games. Predictably the press boys were after me for a comment and I said: 'I'd like to think I have proved I can score goals in the First Division. Hurdles are bound to present themselves again and it is up to me to improve and rise to the standards required. Every goalscorer hits a barren spell every now and again. Next time I hope people will be more understanding and won't say I cannot play in the First Division.' John Hollins, who had provided so much comfort and understanding when things had not been going so well earlier in the season, applied a bit more home-spun psychology by telling the newspapers: 'Kerry still has lots of things to do and learn. All right he got three but it should have been six. There should have been not only more for him but for others as well. If he had chipped the ball over instead of shooting we would have had other goals.'

Perhaps he was entitled to try and ensure I didn't get carried away with either the success or media projection. Conversely, he was careful to offer words of encouragement to my partner David Speedie who had been struggling to find his form. The club had just signed a recognised goalscorer in Gordon Davies from Fulham who had watched the match from the stands. Hollins stressed that Speedie's contribution was invaluable because he drew defenders away from me. I had long since learned to appreciate to the full Speedie's contribution to the team effort in terms of enthusiasm, competitiveness, application and skill and had made a point of telling the press that with Speedie and Pat Nevin beside me goalscoring was a whole lot easier.

There was an amusing moment when Davies reported for his first training session. Unknown to him, he had stripped off and put his clothes on the dressing room peg normally occupied by Speedie. The newspapers had already made a big play of the fact that Davies had been signed to replace Speedie in the team which was to prove totally unfounded speculation. When David walked into the dressing room and observed where Davies had chosen to change into his training gear he blustered: 'Not only are you after my place in the team you've already pinched my peg.' Even Speedie managed to join in the roars of laughter which exploded in the dressing room. But I felt sorry for him nevertheless. His spirits were down and after my own experiences earlier in the season I knew exactly how he was feeling.

My goal in a 1-1 draw at Millwall took us into the third round of the Milk Cup on an aggregate win of 4-2, where our opponents were Walsall. Our first encounter with them, in the week leading up to the Coventry game, had been saved by a goal from our right back, Colin Lee, just five minutes from time, resulting in a replay. There was to be no mistake this time. Walsall had reached the semi-finals of the Milk Cup in the previous season only to be beaten by Liverpool; this time the Third Division club had disposed of Coventry to set up the meeting with us. But they never recovered from a welcome goal from Speedie after just three minutes. I recorded my fourteenth goal of the season three minutes later and by the twelfth minute of the match we were three goals clear following an effort from Keith Jones. The goals continued to flow steadily for me and on 21st November, 1984 I got my second hat-trick of the season in a 4-1 Milk Cup win over Manchester City, which put Chelsea into the quarter-finals of the competition. My second goal was my fiftieth for Chelsea and, at the end of the game, my total had reached seventeen goals in the previous thirteen matches.

There was beginning to be speculation about whether I would be given a chance at international level by the England manager Bobby Robson, but this died down a bit when Robson named as many as sixty players for three international squads and I was not among them. I have to confess that, after my three goals against Manchester City, I was taken aback by the comments of John Hollins – a few words of praise with a sting in the tail – 'The time to judge a player is over a season, not over five minutes,' he said. 'I've seen what publicity can do to players. The less people say the better.' Of course, he was right in what he said, but with my home life and background there was no chance of me being carried away. However, I was comforted to hear Billy McNeill, manager of Manchester City, saying: 'I knew nothing about him when I came down from Scotland but every time I see him he looks the best centre forward in the country.' I felt I still needed to explain my position to the newspapers and I told them: 'I will not let my goals go to my head. I am not a big-head and while my burning ambition is to play for England there is obviously something wrong with my game. I will not feel I have arrived as a player until I have become an England regular.' Hollins, and the rest of the backroom staff at Chelsea, provided a great deal of assistance and advice at a time when there was a danger my head might have been turned by the publicity. But I had known what it was like to really work for a living following my apprenticeship with Cardale Engineering and there was no way I would allow the attention to affect me.

There was much more publicity to follow because I was due to make my first return to Tottenham, the club which had rejected me as a youngster. I harboured no grudge against Spurs but, nevertheless, it was satisfying to score a goal at White Hart Lane after just six minutes. Mark Falco, one of my old rivals in the Tottenham youth team, equalised in the second half with a brilliant header.

The month of November had been memorable and my efforts were rewarded by two personal awards. First there was the *Daily Mirror* Footballer of the Month and then the *London Evening Standard* Footballer of the Month Award. The *Mirror* presented me with a silver salver and a framed drawing of myself which was handed to me on the pitch at Stamford Bridge before our home game against Liverpool on 1st December. Another silver salver followed from the *Standard* plus two magnums of the finest champagne to celebrate a month which had brought ten goals including two hat-tricks.

Alas, it appeared that Bobby Robson remained unimpressed. He had watched me play against Tottenham and was at Stamford Bridge to see me score after ten minutes against Liverpool. I was particularly pleased with the latter goal because I dispossessed Alan Hansen and beat Bruce Grobbelaar with a shot from the outside of my right foot, when I am sure he was expecting me to pass to Speedie or Nevin who were waiting in the middle. Unfortunately, I damaged the ligaments in my right knee in the challenge on Hansen and the fact I was forced to quit before the end of the game tempered the joy of a well deserved 3-1 win over the reigning League Champions. Chelsea had to field a new strike force at Sheffield Wednesday the following week because Speedie was suspended and Derek Johnstone finally got his chance to replace me at centre forward. The team earned a creditable 1-1 draw with Davies scoring on his debut. I returned for the next match and, although it soon became apparent I had not fully recovered from the knee injury, I still managed to get our goal in the 1-1 draw with Stoke.

However, the best performance Chelsea has produced in my time with the club came just three days before Christmas against Everton at Goodison Park – and I didn't even get my name on the scoresheet. Everton were on top of the First Division and we were, at this stage, in sixth position. What a game it was in front of just under 30,000 people. Gordon Davies had retained his place alongside me at the front and scored a marvellous hat-trick with some breathtaking finishing. Captain Colin Pates contributed his only goal of the entire season to give us a memorable 4-3 victory. We had knocked Everton off the top, but it was a sign of their consistent and obvious quality when they regained their position at the summit within a month and accelerated away unchallenged to take the League Championship.

The London derby game with Queens Park Rangers on Boxing Day saw me break my vow of the previous season not to take any more penalties. It's amazing what confidence can do for a player. I was perfectly relaxed when I picked up the ball and belted it past goalkeeper Peter Hucker. Even when we were 2-1 down, with less than ten minutes left, I remained unruffled as we were awarded another penalty and I scored again. My Dad has always insisted I shouldn't take penalties because he believes the striker is on a hiding to nothing. But I'm not so sure he is right. After all, a striker's primary job is to score goals and a penalty award provides for a clear shot at goal from twelve yards. Anyway, John Hollins remarked he was gratified to see me scoring from them both against QPR. In fact, I was to be glad of those goals for, as far as League matches were concerned, I suddenly ran into another barren patch and was forced to endure a further eight full First Division matches before I began a further burst of goalscoring.

The start of the FA Cup competition, as far as Chelsea was concerned, was to provide handsome compensation for my current lack of form. The third round draw, which paired us at home against Third Division Wigan Athletic, looked comfortable enough and we were expected to proceed smoothly into the next round without too much trouble. The playing surface at Stamford Bridge is not perfect at the best of times and with the cold weather in January it was rock hard. Wigan shot into a two goal lead through Paul Jewell and Mike Newell and it looked as though a major upset was on the cards. I was impressed with Wigan, they played good football and deserved their early advantage. We managed to drag ourselves back into the game with goals from David Speedie and

Pat Nevin but none of us was looking forward to a replay on their Springfield Park ground. The adverse weather conditions delayed the replay until 26th January which meant we were faced with three vital games in the space of five days. On 28th January we had to play Sheffield Wednesday in the Milk Cup quarter-finals and when that tie was subsequently drawn we met Wednesday again in a thrilling replay on 30th January.

However, the FA Cup replay was a particularly satisfying day for me because I scored four goals in the 5-0 victory over Wigan. Chelsea's play was irresistable. We were four goals in front by half-time. Speedie, who had an excellent game, put us in front with a header after ten minutes and I struck a straight hat-trick before the interval, the second of the trio from the penalty spot. Wigan's unbeaten home cup record which stretched back to 1966 was well and truly smashed when I got my fourth goal and Chelsea's fifth in the second half. Amazingly, although I had scored four goals on two occasions before, these were my first ever goals in the FA Cup competition. I was chuffed to read the after-match verdict by the Wigan manager Harry McNally. He stated: 'If Mark Hately is worth a million, Dixon is priceless. He is the best centre forward in Britain by a mile.' But I was even more delighted to learn I had cheered up John Neal, still recovering slowly from his major operation. He enthused: 'I've seen some finishing in my time but never anything like that. The day will come when Bobby Robson will have to pick him. It was finishing of the highest order.'

As desperate as I undoubtedly was to attract the attention and admiration of the England manager there was just no time available to dwell on personal glories. We had high hopes of reaching Wembley in the Milk Cup but could only scrape a 1-1 draw against Sheffield Wednesday at Stamford Bridge. The necessity of a replay was strictly my fault as I had missed a penalty which would have taken us through to the semi-finals at the first time of asking. I was upset because I felt I had let down the lads. One minute a hero, the next a villain – that's football. Perhaps Dad had been right about taking penalties after all!

TOP *Division Two's top scorer in 1983-84 and I receive the golden boot award from Luther Blissett.*

BOTTOM *The hat-trick – leading scorer in the Third, Second and First Divisions in successive seasons, though I shared the latter with Gary Lineker.*

David Speedie and I have had our ups and downs, but most of the time we share the delight of scoring and the burden of training.

TOP *The moment arrives. Glenn Hoddle leaves the field and makes way for me to win my first England cap as substitute against Mexico in the Azteca Stadium, June 1985.*

BOTTOM *Battling against Paul Caligiuri and Perry Van Beck of the USA in 1985.*

RIGHT *My strength comes in handy as I struggle with Ditmar Jakobs of West Germany during the first international in which I actually lined up at the start.*

BELOW *It's gone like a dream – manager Bobby Robson waits with me to tell Ken Jones all about my two goals against the West Germans.*

TOP *Captain Bryan Robson urging us on against a German free kick.*
BOTTOM *Bryan Robson at the helm again – this time relaxing in Los Angeles during the 1985 summer tour. John Barnes, Glenn Hoddle, Dave Watson and Terry Fenwick are our companions at sea.*

TOP *I score them and he saves them. I am just glad I don't play against the great Peter Shilton too often or my goals would be far fewer.*

BOTTOM *John O'Neill is beaten but I couldn't find the net and Northern Ireland get to Mexico with a 0–0 draw at Wembley.*

TOP *Monterrey provided good opposition in the build-up to the World Cup. I was pleased to get England's first two goals in Mexico, May 1986.*
BOTTOM *Terry Fenwick and I showing the strain during training at high altitude.*

I hope I will still be wearing an England shirt for the 1990 World Cup Finals in Italy.

The replay at the Hillsborough Stadium was truly breathtaking. Wednesday's ground has been used traditionally as a venue for the big FA Cup semi-finals which are always staged on a neutral ground, but even this magnificent theatre of football had never seen anything quite like the game between Sheffield Wednesday and Chelsea. The home team, backed by terrific vocal support from the 36,509 crowd, ripped us apart in the first half. Wednesday, a big, strong physical team are particularly dangerous from set-piece situations like free kicks and corners. We knew this in advance and yet we fell behind to a couple of thumping headers by Mick Lyons and Lee Chapman contrived from just those kind of situations. We looked dead and buried when Brian Marwood thundered in a third goal before half-time from twenty yards. The entire Chelsea team had been stunned by the sheer ferocity of it all and in the dressing room the talk was more about salvaging our pride than actually winning the match. Surely victory was beyond us now but we were determined not to take the thrashing Wednesday were promising. We decided the only way was to give it a real go right from the re-start. Paul Canoville, the substitute, was sent out for the second half in place of Colin Lee and the enforced decision reaped immediate dividends. I'm told just ten seconds had elapsed in the second period when Paul banged in our first goal after Speedie and I had managed to flick the ball on. There was not the slightest hint of the customary celebration as there was still much work to be done. In the sixty-fourth minute of a pulsating contest I brought us right back into the game with a second goal. Eleven minutes later the irrepressible Mickey Thomas smashed in the equaliser from fifteen yards. The Chelsea fans had taken over now with hardly a sound to be heard from the Wednesday terraces. Then the incredible occurred as Canoville put us in front with five minutes remaining after I had crossed to him from the right. Yet the drama was far from finished. With just one minute left the Sheffield full back, Mel Sterland, made a gallant run into our penalty area, where defender Doug Rougvie stuck out a foot and a penalty was awarded against us. I was hoping and praying that Sterland would miss with the kick. I was still very conscious of the fact that this replay, no matter how exciting and magnificent it had been for players and spectators alike, would not have been necessary if I had scored from the penalty spot in the first game. But the Sheffield Wednesday player made no mistake and I must say I admired his calmness and courage despite the fatigue and disappointment I was feeling. Amazingly, there were no further goals in the half-hour of extra time so the tie went into a second replay. Thank goodness it was not to be decided on a sudden-death penalty shoot-out.

Chairman Ken Bates won the toss for the choice of venue, so it was back to Stamford Bridge on 6th February just two days after our FA Cup fourth round game against Millwall. I'd injured my groin in an intervening League game against Leicester and was a spectator as we plunged to a 3-2 defeat against Millwall. But we retained high hopes of Wembley in the Milk Cup.

Sheffield Wednesday shocked us again with an early goal from Gary Shelton but we came back with a goal from Speedie, created by a superb exhibition of skill from Pat Nevin. He had flicked the ball over Wednesday's defensive wall, run onto it himself, and crossed perfectly for Speedie to score with a header at the far post. Just a few minutes before the end, with extra time looming again, Mickey Thomas scored a tremendous winning goal for Chelsea. Our games against Sheffield Wednesday had always contained that extra bit of spice about them ever since our fight for the Second Division championship so it was extremely gratifying to note that we seemed to just hold the edge over them. All of the players were confident we could now overcome Sunderland in the two-legged semi-final to reach our Wembley goal.

My last League goals had both been penalties in the 2-2 draw with QPR on Boxing Day and it took until 16th March in the 3-1 win at Watford for me to score another First Division goal – and that was a bit of a fluke. John Barnes is still ribbing me about it to this day. I hit the ball hard and low from the left and it seemed the Watford goalkeeper, Tony Coton, was sure to save until the ball hit a piece of uprooted turf and bounced up and over his body into the net. It didn't matter to me how it had gone in. Believe me I needed that goal. The pressure on me during this barren period for League goals had not affected me anywhere near as much as it had earlier in the season. Now I had proved I could score goals in the First Division there was no self-doubt involved. People had accepted that sooner or later I would be back on target again which had hardly been the case at the start of the season. Even so, a striker can never be completely happy unless he is hitting the target with regularity.

The highlight of the season, though promised to be the Milk Cup semi-final against Sunderland. In the event, the match turned out to be a sad anti-climax for us all. We travelled to Roker Park full of hope and optimism but perhaps it was destined not to be our night. For a start, we lost our great defender Joe McLaughlin early on with a dislocated shoulder after he had fallen badly on the bone hard pitch. Colin Lee was soon little more than a passenger after damaging his hamstring and Mickey Thomas was suffering badly from a rib injury. Young Dale Jasper had replaced Joe when the game was still goalless and he conceded a penalty when he handled. To the Chelsea players, in the heat of battle, it had looked like a harmless cross which had struck his hand rather than there being any deliberate intent involved. Sunderland's Colin West, now with Watford, scored with the penalty and in the second half tragedy struck us again. A collision between the unfortunate Jasper and West led to another penalty for Sunderland. This time Eddie Niedzwiecki made a brilliant save in pushing the ball against the post but the rebound went straight to West and, although the Sunderland player mishit his shot, it bounced into the net. That goal just about summed up our luck on a sorry night for Chelsea.

We maintained the belief that we could pull the two goals back in the second leg at Stamford Bridge and, indeed, David Speedie produced an early goal. We pressed hard for the equaliser and perhaps left ourselves a bit too vulnerable at the back. Clive Walker, who had been at Chelsea when I first joined the club, took full advantage and scored a glorious goal for Sunderland with a shot into the top right-hand corner which no goalkeeper on earth could have hoped to reach. There was no point in protecting our defences now and we poured forward in search of the goals which might yet rescue the tie, all to no avail because Walker caught us out again with another goal. Nevin's effort for us was academic as Colin West provided a third for the Wearside team.

Sunderland had beaten us 5-2 on aggregate and we were dreadfully disappointed. They had not been doing too well in the First Division and we had fancied our chances strongly. The form-book so often means nothing in cup football. Sunderland, of course, went on to lose the final at Wembley to Norwich with the final irony that both teams were relegated at the end of the season. In fact, Norwich failed to rescue themselves from the Second Division even though they were to beat Chelsea in the last League game of the season at Stamford Bridge. It was an appalling night, with huge puddles forming on the playing surface. We wanted to win the match so that our final position in the First Division would be fifth which would have meant certain qualification for European football. The fact we were beaten 2-1 meant that Liverpool would have to beat Juventus to win the European Cup for Chelsea to earn qualification. In the event, the dreadful night at the Heysel Stadium in Brussels when so many football supporters were killed led to all of England's clubs being banned from European competition.

All in all it had been a satisfactory and exciting return for Chelsea to First Division combat and I certainly could not complain about the impact I had managed to make. Seven goals in the last thirteen games meant I ended my first season as the joint leading goalscorer on twenty-four First Division goals with Gary Lineker. Gary was a Leicester player then and shortly afterwards was transferred to Everton for £800,000. With eight goals in the Milk Cup and a further four in the FA Cup the grand total had reached thirty-six goals in my first season of First Division football. It meant that for the third successive season I had captured the coveted Adidas 'Golden Boot' award for the leading goalscorer and had become the first ever player to win the award in three divisions of the Football League. Surely, not even my biggest critic could complain about that achievement, and yet I was far from convinced I had succeeded in impressing one man above all others . . . England manager Bobby Robson.

ENGLAND AGONIES

I lost count of the number of times Bobby Robson came to watch me play for Chelsea in the 1984-85 season. Everytime he planned to take another look the newspapers were full of it and I admit the situation got to me. I was desperate to play for my country and spent countless hours engrossed in private thoughts of exactly how I could convince the England manager I was worthy of at least an opportunity to become an international player.

The spectre of Robson sitting in the stands scrutinising my play began to haunt me. Everytime he came to watch I would give a poor account of myself and whispers began to reach me that he admired my goalscoring ability but was not so captivated with other aspects of my play. The plethora of rumours and counter-rumours became incessant: some said my technique was suspect, others my touch wasn't good enough; one journalist wrote that if my first touch was unimpressive my final one was devastating!

Speculation in the press was unrelenting, and I didn't think this was helping me in the slightest. I didn't know Robson at all but had heard that he was an honest, decent, open character who cared passionately about the England football team, and the fact that in the previous three years of his tenure as England manager he had been willing to give every potential international player an opportunity to prove himself kept up my spirits. The newspapers devoured voraciously every available word on the subject, one national daily producing a gigantic headline which proclaimed: 'Tug-of-War for Dixon.' They'd got wind of the fact that I was also qualified to play for either the Republic of Ireland or Wales at international level as, although I had been born in Luton, both of my Dad's parents came from the Republic of Ireland and my mother's father had been born in Wales. It was all nonsense really. The facts were right enough but England and only England was the country I wanted to represent at international level. I was concerned that the pressure being exerted by the press might cause Robson to dig in his heels and insist he would not be moved, and was very much aware that it was up to me, and me alone, to prove to him that I was worth a chance. If there was a breakthrough, I feel sure it came in an exciting game against Liverpool at Anfield on 4th May, 1985.

It was a marvellous match and Chelsea played superbly as a team to come back from 3-1 down at half-time only to lose 4-3. I'd scored one of the goals and had been well pleased with my overall contribution. The extrovert Liverpool goalkeeper, Bruce Grobbelaar, commented after the game: 'It's silly that Dixon is not in the England squad. In my opinion he should be in the team itself. He's better than the others in there. He's a big lad who works hard, sets things up for his colleagues and scores goals.' It would be false modesty to suggest I didn't enjoy reading such words from my professional colleagues, but still nothing was heard from Bobby Robson. John Neal stuck his oar in by telling the press: 'They said he wouldn't score goals in the Second Division but he did. They said he wouldn't score them in the First Division but he has. They say he won't get goals in international football, but believe me Dixon will.'

The England manager was due to name a squad of players who would travel to Finland for an important World Cup qualifying game, before returning to Britain for the domestic international with Scotland at Hampden Park. The same players would then travel to Mexico for a summer tournament involving games against Mexico, Italy and West Germany before finishing off with a friendly match against the United States in Los Angeles. It was a tense time for me but I was heartened by words from Bobby Robson, spoken the day before he was to reveal his selection, when he compared me to the great West German striker Gerd Muller: 'It is difficult to ignore any player from the First Division who scores that many goals. There is a lot of suggestion that Dixon lacks real finesse but then they used to say that about Gerd Muller and look what he achieved.'

I still had to pinch myself when the squad was finally announced and my name was in it. Robson reasoned the only way to discover if I could produce the goals at international level was to give me the chance to do it. That had always been my attitude. I knew I would be a mere apprentice among the best footballers in England. I was going to learn a lot in the coming weeks and I must admit I was both anxious and apprehensive when I joined the squad at the Chiltern Hotel in Luton on the night before we were due to leave for the game in Finland. I need not have been so concerned. The lads in the squad were warm and friendly with Chris Waddle, Terry Butcher and Kenny Sansom particularly welcoming. It was early to bed that night in time for an early start for Finland from Luton Airport the following morning.

At the airport Bobby Robson pulled me to one side, congratulated me on my selection, and asked if I would mind playing for the England Under-21 team on the night before the big World Cup qualifying match. He explained he was short of strikers for the Under-21 game and I could qualify to play as an over-age player under the rules of the European Championship competition. Mr Robson added he had not contemplated playing me in the big match because it was important I should settle down first as a member of the squad itself and, in any event, Mark Hateley was at that stage his number one centre forward. I was delighted to comply with the request. I had not played for an England representative team at any level of competition and the very fact I would be wearing an England shirt for the first time in my life was more than enough incentive. I considered selection by the Under-21 team as the first step on the ladder of international experience.

It seemed to me I was included in the squad because of the

sheer volume of goals I had produced during the previous season with Chelsea rather than outstanding performances when Mr Robson had been watching me play. This concerned me slightly as perhaps I had attempted things I would not normally have contemplated in an effort to impress, instead of concentrating on my normal, natural game. It had been difficult for me because I had always been aware that Mr Robson was at the match. It appeared the England manager knew of my anxiety because he commented in the press: 'Maybe it is a good job I haven't seen every game Kerry's played this season otherwise he might have scored only seven rather than thirty-six goals.'

I considered my selection for the Under-21 team as a vital part of the learning process. There were some good players in the team: Stewart Robson of Arsenal, and West Ham's Tony Cottee who went on to make a considerable name for himself as a goalscorer in the 1985-86 season. However, things didn't go too well for the team. The match was played in a remote town called Mikkeli and we were two goals in arrears after only seventeen minutes. The moment I had been waiting for arrived in the fifty-fourth minute. The Sunderland player, Nick Pickering, now with Coventry City, crossed perfectly and I was able to volley a shot into the far corner of the net. Unfortunately, Finland got another goal shortly before the end and the 3-1 defeat didn't look too good at all, expecially when we learnt it had been Finland's first ever victory over England at any level. However, I was encouraged greatly by the reaction of Dave Sexton, the manager in charge of the England Under-21 team, who told me he thought I had done well in my first representative game and had taken my goal splendidly. It was a great boost to hear those words from as highly respected a coach as Sexton. Despite the result I had enjoyed the entire experience and was now relishing the prospect of joining up with the full England squad for the game at Hampden Park and the summer tour.

Although Mr Robson's doubts about my ability to prosper at international level continued to fuel endless speculation on the sports pages I had no cause for complaint about the way he and the players welcomed me back into the fold. The manager seemed keen enough to ensure I was made to feel one of the family. I watched the World Cup qualifying game from a seat in the stands and although I was playing no part in the match, either as a performer or a substitute, I still felt very much part of the team. Mark Hateley, my most direct rival, got the goal which gave England a satisfactory 1-1 draw. There was no resentment from me, I cheered as loudly and felt as chuffed as anyone. There was an atmosphere of togetherness in this squad which was to prosper further in Mexico and America. To be frank, I was surprised by the open friendliness demonstrated by all of the players. So often when football teams get together, especially when they are drawn from so many different clubs, little cliques form in groups of two and threes. I was assured by the other players that kind of thing had not occurred under the management of Mr Robson and it was obviously something he had guarded against. This team spirit was the marvellous asset of the squad of players who prepared for the 1986 World Cup, so much so that when Hateley scored it never even entered my head that his success might blight the advancement of my own international career. I was merely elated by the fact the goal had put us one step closer to qualification for the World Cup Finals.

The party flew back to Troon to prepare for the game against Scotland but the international against the auld enemy turned out to be a bit of a let down for us all. I was named as one of the substitutes and at one stage during the game I was instructed to begin my warm-up routine. For one marvellous moment I thought I might be going on, but the decision was to withdraw Glenn Hoddle and send out Trevor Francis. In the end we were all disappointed because Scotland claimed victory with a fine header from Richard Gough.

We were allowed to return home to our families for just a couple of days before reporting once more to the Post House Hotel at London Heathrow for the long journey to Mexico City. Personally, I couldn't wait for the time to arrive. The manager had told all of the players that everyone would be given at least one game. The Italian-based players, Mark Hateley, Ray Wilkins and Trevor Francis, were required to return to their clubs after the second game of the tour against Mexico because they had been ordered to play in the Italian Cup competition.

I don't think I'll ever forget one of the first training sessions conducted in the heat and altitude of Mexico. We ended with a twelve minute run which proved absolutely exhausting for all of us. My long distance record, even in the normal conditions of home, had proved to be far from outstanding, so I expected to be at the back of the field. Thankfully, I wasn't the only player who struggled to come to terms with the conditions. Everton's Gary Stevens soon proved to be a natural athlete and he led the field with Bryan Robson, Dave Watson of Norwich and Watford's John Barnes in close attendance. No one was more surprised than me to finish the session in the middle of the pack. The run had certainly proved its purpose to us all. Previously, the horrors of heat and altitude had been a daunting theory, but now we had practical experience of the difficulties. Breathing was particularly hard, your throat so constricted that you had to fight for every gasp of air. Even a gentle jog up the stairs of the hotel proved exerting, so how we had managed to keep going for a full twelve minutes I will never know. However, the 600 metre sprints were the absolute killers. After each burst the England doctor, Vernon Edwards, and the coaching staff would check the pulse to measure the recovery rate from strenuous activity. We also had to undergo plenty of blood and urine tests, our body weight was checked constantly and our food intake carefully monitored and supplemented with iron and salt tablets.

The entire squad went to watch the World Champions, Italy play the World Cup hosts, Mexico in the magnificent Azteca Stadium. The accommodation for spectators is superb and the entire vista quite breathtaking. We were to discover later that the dressing rooms are not nearly as sumptuous and when we used them they were always flooded with water! The Italians looked a good team to me. They had been in Mexico for some time, having already played a couple of games against club teams, so were fully acclimatised to the conditions and would no doubt prove difficult opponents for England in the mini-tournament. All of the England players were entranced by the actions of the home supporters which I can only describe as synchronised acclaim for their team. The Azteca Stadium holds 120,000 people, all of them are seated, and one after the other the supporters rise from those seats with arms upraised and quickly sit down again. The result is a spectacular human wave which gets faster and faster as it builds up around the stadium.

We had learned from our training sessions, conducted at a pleasant country club in the hills above Mexico City, that because of the thinner air the ball would travel further and faster than we were accustomed to at home. Therefore, when practising, I concentrated on getting up that little bit earlier so that I was, in effect, waiting for the ball in the air when it was crossed in my direction. This tactic was to pay rich dividends for me later in the tour.

Our game against Italy was hardly a memorable occasion. Mark Hateley had once again cheered us all with a fine goal which looked enough to give us an honourable draw, when the Italians were awarded a ridiculous penalty by the Mexican referee in the dying minutes of the game. The game was lost undeservedly but all of the players had been heartened by the first performance in the inclement conditions. As each day passed we were aware that our bodies were becoming more in tune with the conditions. The team played reasonably well in the game against Mexico and were unfortunate to lose the match by the only goal. Even so, Mexico had shown us enough to suggest they could be a major force on their own territory when the World Cup Finals got underway.

The Italian players returned to their clubs and once again the speculation heightened as to whether I would get my first full appearance. I had been sent on by Mr Robson for the final seven minutes of the game against Mexico with the simple instructions to do what I could which, I'm afraid, wasn't much but I was so pleased to have actually got out there on the pitch.

To be honest, I had not pinned my hopes on playing in the third match of our tour against West Germany, but, as speculation increased in the press, I must admit I began to wish secretly I might be included in the team. Mr Robson's assurance that all the players would be given one full game had led me to believe that I would play in the final fixture against the USA in Los Angeles, so when the official word came that I was to be given my first full international appearance against West Germany I was walking on air.

The newspaper lads hunted me down but I was determined there would be no irresponsible boasts from me and wanted to maintain a low profile. If the chances came my way I would hope to take them but in the meantime there had to be no irrelevent proclamations, predictions or forecasts. Many people had suggested I would not be a success at international level. Now I was about to discover for myself. No one needed to tell me this was going to be a big day in my professional life. I was nervous all right but not as badly as I had envisaged. Mind you, I think if I had been aware at the time of the demands being made in the newspapers back in England I might have been trembling in my boots. Bobby Robson was quoted as saying: 'He's been chucked in at the deep end and he has to swim,' adding: 'Kerry must not try to do the things he cannot do. He must concentrate on what he is good at. There is a big difference between international and club football. And he'll be playing against a system he has never confronted.'

England had a lot to live down as the team had not won in four games, having lost the three previous matches, and we were later to learn that no England team has ever lost four successive games. The night before I telephoned my Dad at home in Luton. He counselled me to stick strictly to what I did best and told me it was important to play my normal game, to pass the ball simply and accurately and, if goalscoring opportunities came my way, to concentrate strongly on keeping my cool.

It is impossible to describe adequately the overwhelming sense of pride I felt when I pulled the England shirt over my head in the dressing room before the game. I'd had seven minutes as a substitute, of course, in the previous game against Mexico but this was entirely different. This time I would be involved from the start. Against Mexico I had been given no time to think, no time to digest the great honour about to be bestowed on me. Now I could sit and reflect on a wildly fluctuating career which was about to reach its height. Most boys with a love of football have at some time or other harboured dreams and enacted fantasies of stardom. For all too brief moments they have believed they are Bobby Charlton, Tom Finney, Stanley Matthews, Bobby Moore or Geoff Hurst. But as the National Anthem sounded around the vast Azteca Stadium I was very much aware that, at the age of twenty-three years and eleven months, I was at long last Kerry Dixon of England. This was no dream.

The early pace of the game was hectic and it seemed that Gary Lineker and I were making a lot of runs without actually receiving the ball. The breakthrough arrived when Glenn Hoddle sought me out with a nicely judged chip pass. From the corner of my eye I saw Bryan Robson begin one of those characteristic runs of his into space and instinctively I chested the ball down into his path. About a minute earlier the captain had been guilty of a missed opportunity to put us ahead when he had scooped his chance over the crossbar, but this time there was to be no mistake. His finishing was superb and it was a marvellous moment for me, too, in having contributed to a very good English goal.

The West German team had arrived in Mexico only a couple of days before the game subscribing to the theory that the altitude problem has little effect in so short a time. For a while it looked as though they might be right as they rained in spectacular shots from all angles, and Peter Shilton had to be at his most vigilant. Shortly before half-time the Germans were presented with a golden opportunity to level the game when Mark Wright pulled down Uwe Rahn. But the magnificent Shilton dived to his left and saved brilliantly the penalty from Andreas Brehme. Some of the England lads required a quick whiff of oxygen at half-time to relieve the aching lungs but as I was feeling in great shape and ready for another forty-five minutes I didn't bother. Just eight minutes of the second half had elapsed when I was celebrating the most unforgettable moment of my life. Terry Butcher pushed forward into an attacking position robbing Klaus Augenthaler and thundered towards the West German penalty area. I raced forward in support and, as Butcher attempted to go round Harald Schumacher, the goalkeeper touched the ball in my direction. I had an empty goal in front of me but the ball had come at me sharply and for one horrible moment got clogged up under my feet before I was able to knock it towards the goal. I didn't see the ball actually cross the line because I had already wheeled away in sheer excitement and wasn't aware, until later, that the shot had grazed the inside of the post before going in. Some people said they thought I had missed, but I knew it was a goal from the moment I hit the shot.

The West Germans were finished, many of them appearing to have reached the point of physical exhaustion. Then in the sixty-seventh minute even my own wildest dreams were exceeded. John Barnes, my roommate on the tour, had replaced Lineker who had been forced to go off because of cramp. John put over a superb cross to the far post, the hours of practice in jumping that split-second earlier than normal to allow for the atmospheric conditions paying off handsomely. I was up there waiting when the ball arrived and was able to power a header well beyond the West German goalkeeper. A second goal, I just couldn't believe it. It was like a dream. I kept expecting to wake up at any moment. I could imagine the scenes in the living room of Mum and Dad's house back home in Luton, of them dancing in delight round the television. The rest of the game is now a blurr; all I know is the Germans were well and truly beaten.

Coming off the field at the end I was grabbed by a television interviewer who asked me to describe my feelings. I told him I was over the moon, and got some stick about that from the lads a bit later. It's become the footballer's catch phrase now and most of us consciously try to avoid it, but at that moment it summed up exactly how I was feeling. We had completed the biggest win over West Germany for fifty years, more comprehensive even than in the 1966 World Cup Final at Wembley. All of the team were elated and although the manager didn't go overboard we could all tell how pleased he was inside. He just said to me: 'Well done, son.' As soon as we returned to the hotel I telephoned Mum and Dad who couldn't disguise their happiness, but Mum said Dad was suffering from a headache. Apparently he'd been even more nervous than me!

The England party was in great heart as we moved off to Los Angeles. The victory over West Germany had provided welcome relief for us all and it was said the game against the USA would be much easier although I certainly didn't see it that way. As far as I was concerned the team was on a hiding to nothing: if we were beaten we would be crucified in the press and if we won by a couple of goals it would still be classed as a disappointing result. We were all very much aware of the importance of ending the tour on the right note and from the moment Gary Lineker put us ahead with a quite astonishing goal – a magnificent shot on the volley – the result was never in doubt. I was lucky enough to score another two goals in the eventual 5-0 victory and I could have possibly ended up with four if I'd taken all of my chances. 'Well done, son, you've had a great tour,' said Bobby Robson as the party left the hotel on Sunset Boulevard to return to England. The manager was staying behind in America to visit Colorado in the hope of establishing our training headquarters before the start of the 1986 World Cup Finals. I was gratified to read his comments in the newspapers when I returned to England. He said: 'We didn't really know Kerry before he came on this trip but he has impressed everyone with his attitude. He's a nice lad and an excellent tourist. He has shown he can get goals at this level and providing he can continue his goalscoring form next season he looks the ideal back-up at centre forward.'

I felt great satisfaction in having proved certain people wrong. On occasions the criticism had been hurtful and unfair, but I knew that even though I had shown I could score goals at the highest level, there was still a long way for me to go. I had executed the breakthrough and it was up to me to build on it. My ambition to play for England had been achieved and now I had to concentrate totally on returning to Mexico the following year as a fully-fledged member of the World Cup squad. I knew that long after the sun-tan had faded and the newspaper clippings curled up the memory of my first taste of international football with England would remain vivid, but I could afford to take nothing for granted and was determined to sample more of it. Four goals from two full appearances and another in the England Under-21 game had taken my total for the entire season to forty-one. I admit I was fairly happy with that little lot.

Yet, I confess to being disappointed when I was not a member of the team in the first two internationals of the 1985-86 season – in fact, I was not even named as a substitute. A draw against Rumania at Wembley plus a 5-0 win over Turkey kept England on course for World Cup qualification. There was no explanation forthcoming as to why I had been omitted by the manager and none was expected. I was a member of a squad of highly-skilled players and that was good enough for me. But after the game against Turkey Mr Robson took me aside and told me he intended to pick me in the team for the final World Cup qualifier against Northern Ireland. He believed I needed the experience of playing at Wembley and had kept me off the substitutes bench in previous matches because he wanted me to play from the start of the match. Even though Mark Hateley was injured shortly before the game I believe the manager would have stuck by his word no matter what.

I had never played at Wembley so it was the realisation of another dream. What an experience it proved to be – and I am not just talking about actually playing in the hallowed stadium. I was chastised in the press for missing a couple of chances and had also been let down badly by the media before the game. When it was announced that I was in the team the journalists flocked around eagerly to ask me questions. I was on my guard, determined to maintain a low profile. Northern Ireland had to avoid defeat to ensure that they, too, would qualify for the World Cup Finals and as England were already sure of a place the eyes of the world were watching the situation for any sign of a fix between the two home countries. 'The Irish need a point and you need to play well to enhance your claims,' stated one journalist. 'Yes,' I replied, 'That's right.' Then came. 'It would break Pat Jennings heart if he was to lose out now,' said another journalist. 'I suppose it would,' I replied. I'd spotted the line they were after and was determined to say no more.

Pat Jennings, one of the all time greats of goalkeeping, was bidding to reach the World Cup Finals in his forty-first year, thus providing a romantic enough story without any need for embroidery. Even though I had been able to detect the tone of the conversation I still couldn't believe the headlines screaming out of the so-called popular tabloid newspapers the next morning. 'I'll break Jennings heart vows Dixon,' said one. 'I'll break Irish hearts vows Dixon' said another. I cringed with embarrassment. I had definitely said nothing like that and, in fact, had done my utmost to avoid it. I was so disgusted by the headlines that I was reluctant to join the other players for breakfast, though surely they wouldn't believe I would have said something like that. I was also upset because I had liked and trusted a couple of the reporters, but now they had ruined our good relationship forever. Now some of them complain that Kerry Dixon is a hard man to get to know. The situation will remain that way. I have always defended the right of any journalists to his opinions and even admire those among them who do not rate me as a player simply because they are honest and have had the guts to say so to my face and explain their reasons. But I cannot and will not forgive those who besmirched my name with the headlines that morning.

Fortunately, my Irish friends knew me well enough to realise I would never say anything like that. Sometime later I met up with Pat Jennings at a charity function and apologised to him for what had appeared and assured him I had said none of these things. He told me not to worry any further and explained he'd been in the game long enough to know that all professional players are susceptible to the manipulations of certain journalists anxious to create a sensational headline.

The game, itself, hadn't gone much better for me as I missed a couple of chances. A beautiful pass from Glenn Hoddle gave me the opportunity to get in a header but instead of glancing the ball I tried to power it beyond Jennings and was woefully wide. In the second half I had another opportunity to score. The ball had spun into the air off a defender and was dropping down over my left-hand shoulder. As it landed the vicious spin caused the ball to shoot away off the surface and I failed to connect. I know it looked bad but, in all honesty, I can say it was one of the most difficult goalscoring chances I had been faced with in my entire career and it would have been almost impossible to score even if I had connected. However, I'm prepared to hold up my hands and concede it was a miss. Any thought I had of making amends was denied by Jennings. I was certain I had scored the goal which would have won us the match and turned Northern Ireland away from Mexico when I rose at the far post to meet a centre from Gary Stevens. I connected perfectly with my forehead and Jennings looked hopelessly beaten, but somehow he arched his back and touched the ball over the crossbar with his outstretched hand – a truly amazing piece of goalkeeping. I don't know about me breaking his heart, he'd certainly succeeded in damaging mine!

My feelings were mixed after that game. I was dreadfully disappointed at missing the opportunities to increase my international goal tally but at the same time delighted Northern Ireland had joined England in qualifying for the World Cup Finals. I had already been left out of the squad to prepare for a friendly international against Egypt, in Cairo, because Chelsea were involved in a vital Milk Cup tie against Liverpool. It was unfortunate because I had been anxious to make amends for the lapses against the Irish but as it turned out I was even more unlucky in the cup game sustaining a bad injury which was to threaten my place in the squad for the World Cup Finals itself.

A fortnight before the next international date in Israel Bobby Robson contacted me to inquire if I would be fit enough to be selected for the squad. The doctor had told me that I should be recovered sufficiently to be able to play, if selected, but even then the level of match fitness I could acquire was debatable. On the Thursday before the squad was due to assemble I was aware my fitness was doubtful and contemplated withdrawing from the England party altogether in terms of playing in the match, although at the same time requesting that I travel with the party because I very much wanted to remain a part of the England set-up. It transpired that Bobby Robson had been involved in deep discussions with the Chelsea manager John Hollins as to whether I would be fit enough to withstand the rigours of an international game. He'd asked Hollins if Chelsea would have been prepared to play me in a First Division match on the night England were due to play in Tel Aviv, Hollins replying that he would have selected me if that had been the case. It seemed this answer was good enough for the England manager.

I was in a turmoil: some friends advised me to play while others were concerned I might be risking my entire international career by attempting to prove my worth when I was nowhere near one hundred per cent fitness. On the Sunday night I reported to the England team hotel at Luton and went immediately to Mr Robson's room. I told him I was not match fit, and he assured me he was well aware of the situation but still believed it was important for me to take part in the game. He stressed it would not influence him in any way as far as the future was concerned if I was unable to complete the match. I returned to my own room to mull over the situation on my own. I was far from happy with the circumstances but such was my determination to play for England I knew I had to go out to Israel and do my best. Besides, I was very much aware another striker was beginning to exert pressure on my place in the England squad.

Mick Harford, of Luton Town, had been enjoying some spectacular publicity and the press appeared to be launching a similar campaign on his behalf to the one which had helped squeeze me into the squad. The Luton manager at the time, David Pleat was forever extolling the virtues of Harford in the columns of the national newspapers. There was no doubt that Harford had enjoyed an outstanding season, and I was aware of his desire to play for England as we had met on several occasions in Luton. His major asset is his prodigious heading ability and he possesses a delicate touch for such a big man. But he lacks my speed and eye for the opportunist type of goal. Nevertheless, he was a threat to my position and I was aware that if I should drop out of the squad through injury on this occasion he would more than likely be given his chance. I couldn't afford to take that kind of risk and as the manager was insistent on me not only making the trip to Israel but also playing in the match I believed I was left with little alternative but to go.

The weather in Israel provided a marvellous contrast to what we had been experiencing at home during that period. League matches were being postponed in abundance through ice and snow back in England while we were basking in the warm sunshine and even contemplating a spell of sunbathing on the beach outside the hotel. However, I was far from comfortable with my own situation, and was very worried about my fitness in the training session held on the Monday before the game. The injury had been a bad one, the muscles around the pelvis having been wrenched away from the bone, and everytime I attempted to make a quick run I was terrified that it might go again. I was running freely enough though, and figured that every day the situation would improve. Unfortunately, from the very first minute of the match I was conscious of the restriction in my mobility. How ever much training a player does, match conditions are very different and as I struggled through the opening half I knew I was a shadow of my real self.

The Israeli team had caught us out with a shock goal in the early minutes and, with Peter Beardsley playing alongside me in his first full international because of injury to Gary Lineker, we were not making much impact. Bryan Robson levelled the scores with a stupendous right foot volley from a marvellous pass by Glenn Hoddle and shortly afterwards I was taken off. Captain Robson rescued victory for us late in the game from a penalty after his own goalbound header had been handled on the line by an Israeli defender.

I didn't know what to think. I wasn't sure one way or the other as to whether I had been wise to agree to play in the game and the manager certainly eased my mind on the five hour flight back to Luton immediately after the game. He pulled me to one side and insisted that I had not damaged my international prospects by taking part when not fully fit. He assured me I would be named in his next squad for a tough international against Russia in the USSR and added that he was definitely a man of his word. Unfortunately, the final of the Full Members Cup Competition was scheduled to take place at Wembley between Chelsea and Manchester City on the Sunday preceeding the Wednesday date of the international game against Russia, so the England manager had no alternative but to acceed to Chelsea's request that I be made available to them to play in the game. As Mark Hateley and Gary Lineker would again be the first choice strikers for England Mr Robson obviously had to comply. As it turned out Hateley was ruled out of the match through injury while I picked up a knock in the Saturday League game against Southampton and was not available to play in the Cup Final. Thankfully Mr Robson again chose to ignore the strengthening claims of Luton's Harford as a replacement.

However, a new threat was presented in the brilliant performances of Lineker and Peter Beardsley at the front. Neither was physically equipped to play the role of the conventional big target men but their explosive running provided different attacking dimensions. It was Beardsley who set up a winning goal with a marvellous tackle on the edge of the Russian penalty area before placing the ball in the path of Chris Waddle to score. The result was undoubtedly a major landmark from England's point of view as the Russians had not been beaten in a major international football match on their own soil for seven years. Too many names for comfort were now in contention for the squad of twenty-two players that Bobby Robson would nominate to compete in the World Cup Finals. I had begun to get nervous about my own prospects and was so desperate to go to Mexico I found myself making out lists of players and attempting to settle on a final twenty-two names. It would be vital to be a member of the squad nominated to play Scotland at Wembley in the oldest international fixture of all as Mr Robson was pledged to name his World Cup squad on the Monday following the Scotland game.

The England manager stood by the word he had given me on that return trip from Israel. I was named in the squad for the Scotland game but knew that if Mark Hateley and Gary Lineker were fit I would be on the substitutes bench. In the event, Lineker was injured when playing for Everton and for a while there was conjecture that I would be selected to play alongside Hateley. I was quite happy about the prospect even though some of the so-called experts believed the two of us would be unable to form an effective striking partnership because we were similar types of players. To my mind Hateley was not the only opponent I was up against in my ambition to become a regular member of the England team, though it appeared to have become accepted universally that the two of us were big rivals for the same position. However, I maintain that Hateley is not a natural goal-scorer which is my main asset. The only time I have ever come up against him was in a match for Chelsea against Portsmouth in the Second Division. I got a stack of goals that season and Chelsea were promoted while Portsmouth stayed down. I don't know if the goals I scored and the goals Hateley didn't were a contributory factor or not to our selection. But there are the facts. In the summer, at the end of that season, Hateley was chosen by England to go on the South American tour and scored a superbly headed goal in a memorable victory. Shortly afterwards he was signed by AC Milan, from Portsmouth, for £1 million.

When I was first called upon to join the England squad I was a bit apprehensive about what Hateley's reaction would be as, after all, we were rivals for the same position. But he was both charming and friendly, and impressed me immediately as a normal down-to-earth type with similar ambitions to my own. His Dad, Tony Hateley, played as a professional and had obviously exerted a major influence on his professional career so we have much in common. The two of us are very much aware that we are rivals but there has been no attempt to create any kind of antagonist atmosphere between the two of us and we are both determined to allow our performances on the field of play to do the talking for us.

Trevor Francis was called up for the game against Scotland to play his first international for almost a year on an occasion which proved to be a trial by ordeal for him. A succession of injuries had blighted his international career and the Scotland game would provide his final opportunity to clinch a place in the World Cup squad. I felt sorry for Trevor as the pressure on him was enormous and although he played well he failed to score. England beat Scotland 2-1 which was as good a result as any to send us on our way to Mexico, the goals scored by Terry Butcher and Glenn Hoddle, thus confirming England's ninth successive game without defeat. I was on the substitutes bench and was not called upon to play.

Now the real sweat was about to begin. In just six days the final squad would be named by the manager. The original plan had been for Mr Robson to name twenty-eight players to travel to Colorado in America for the World Cup preparation, with six players released on the 25th May deadline when the final composition of the squad had to be lodged with FIFA. But the manager decided to alter his plan. He would name the final twenty-two with six other players on stand-by in case of injuries before the deadline. These six players would remain in England, in full training, ready to fly out in case of emergency.

There was much speculation in the press after the Scotland game with one or two newspapers claiming to have printed the names of the actual twenty-two players. My name was among them but I refused to take anything for granted. When the day of reckoning arrived I was a bundle of nerves. But there it was. Kerry Dixon was going to Mexico. It was a huge relief. I felt terribly sorry for the good players who had been omitted – Tony Woodcock and Trevor Francis especially had provided England with sterling service. Trevor Francis complained bitterly to the newspapers about the way he had been treated. It was easy to sympathise as I knew just how devastated I would have been if my name had not been among the chosen few. On the day before the international against Scotland all of the players had been measured for World Cup suits and I can remember thinking at the time that if I was left out of the squad I would be unable to recover from the sheer embarrassment.

Even so, I knew I would not completely believe I was going to Mexico until I had actually set foot on the aircraft on the morning of 7th May. Chelsea's last game of the season was against Watford on 5th May and with this fixture safely negotiated we were on our way. I couldn't wait. No matter what was to occur I just knew this would be the proudest moment of my life.

HARSH PROFESSIONAL LIFE

While the 1985-86 campaign concluded happily for me, in that I earned my place in the squad as one of England's twenty-two players for the World Cup in Mexico, the season itself was very much a mixed bag of highs and lows.

On my return from Mexico and the United States in the summer of 1985 I was able to snatch a three-week break before the start of the new season. Much had occurred at Chelsea during my absence. John Hollins, who had proved to be a coach of considerable ability following a long and distinguished career as a player, had been appointed team manager in place of John Neal. Mr Neal had continued his steady progress to renewed health and vigour after open-heart surgery the previous summer, but it seemed advisable to allow him to escape from the rigours of day to day involvement and to draw on his vast depth of experience by installing him in an advisory position. I confess I was deeply disappointed. While John Hollins had most certainly earned his promotion and I had no quarrel with his actual appointment, John Neal will always command a special respect in my affections. He was the manager who had taken a chance on me when I was scoring goals for Reading in the Third Division. Many had taken a look at me but none had the courage of their convictions except Mr Neal, whose tremendous faith in me has, I believe, encouraged me to become a better player. I owe Mr Neal a great deal and I'm not the kind of bloke who is likely to forget the fact. Other players at Chelsea had similar cause to be thankful for John Neal. When he was re-building Chelsea Football Club he backed his judgement and provided many of the current team with an opportunity they might not otherwise have enjoyed to make it to the top of their profession.

Earlier that year, in March 1985, I had signed a new four-year contract with Chelsea even though my existing agreement still had more than a year to run. Negotiations had been conducted with the chairman Ken Bates on his magnificent farm at Beaconsfield, and although relations were always amicable between us we were unable to reach agreement on the precise nature of the terms. The situation had reached deadlock until Mr Neal stepped in and put a series of proposals to me. I asked for twenty-four hours to think things over and the following day suggested counter-proposals of my own. In fact, the terms of the new contract were eventually sealed by a simple handshake between the manager and I as we sat in his car outside Chelsea's training headquarters close to Heathrow Airport.

Mr Neal was undoubtedly the major reason why I had decided to commit myself to the club for such a long period of time. I liked and I trusted him and you cannot place a price on that kind of relationship. Also Chelsea, I believed, were moving in the right direction; I liked the chairman and got on tremendously well with the players. My concern at the apparent demise of John Neal was not influenced in any way by the fact that John Hollins was taking over as manager, but I knew I was going to miss John Neal for his help, friendship, guidance and wisdom. As a coach, John Hollins had proved refreshing, innovative and enthusiastic. He's a vibrant, ambitious, character and these qualities greatly appeal to me. He could so easily proceed to become a truly great manager. Hollins had brought in Ernie Walley as his coach, who for a brief period had been manager at Crystal Palace. He prided himself on his fitness and toughness and all the Chelsea players were about to discover those attributes were in no way exaggerated.

The new manager telephoned me at home and congratulated

me warmly on the success I had achieved with England during the summer tour. The players were due to report back for pre-season training on a Friday before leaving for the customary purgatory in Aberystwyth on the following Tuesday. I was allowed to miss the Friday get-together and reported to Stamford Bridge on the Monday. The moment I walked through the door the lads were bombarding me with daunting tales about Ernie Walley's philosophies. 'Training is a nightmare,' they insisted. 'The bloke is a Sergeant-Major,' they went on. All this after just one day! Ernie said hello to me and we all set off for a training session down at Battersea Park. One of the exercises devised by Ernie was to pick up a teammate off the floor and raise him off the ground. He chose Doug Rougvie as his guinea pig, who weighs in at fourteen stone plus. He succeeded in lifting Doug, which suggested to me that here was a man prepared to lead by example.

The following day it was off to Aberystwyth, a place which holds bad memories for me after my first visit there for pre-season training following my transfer from Reading to Chelsea. Boy was it tough. I was in reasonably good shape because I'd been in training throughout the summer because of international commitments, but the first session exhausted me as usual. Two runs around the sand dunes and my legs had gone. I collapsed in a heap, gasping for air. Ernie stood above me bellowing that I should get up immediately to aid my recovery. He wanted me to stand up and walk around. It was impossible. My legs just wouldn't do it. I wasn't alone, all of the other lads were in the same boat. I was amazed I had enough energy to collapse! I don't know of any player who actually enjoys pre-season training. It's an absolute necessity, vital to the physical condition required to face a long hard season and once the body has attained a certain level of fitness the rest is reasonably easy. That's why when the season gets underway the training is designed to maintain peak fitness rather than attain it.

Ernie was tough all right and a strict disciplinarian. Early on in the season he took me to one side after a training session and told me that with hard work plus his advice and backing he could make me a permanent fixture in the England team. He insisted I needed plenty of practice in holding up the ball, shielding it from defenders and quick turning. After this conversation it seemed that Ernie was always looking to pick on me for extra work. I was the one who was always singled out. It began to get to me and I became irritated and suspicious. There is no doubt in my mind now that I had misinterpreted his motives and objectives but at the time I found it difficult to remain silent. In the end, I couldn't contain myself any longer and requested a meeting with him after training had finished. I asked him straight out if he rated me as a footballer. He was taken aback by the question. His reply was emphatic. He told me he rated me very highly and when I followed up by demanding to know why he always appeared to be picking on me the answer was straight from the shoulder: 'Because you're a lazy so and so that's why,' he retorted. 'You have got everything going for you but you have got to work hard to attain the highest levels.'

I'm the kind of person who reacts favourably to straight talking. I don't like two-faced people and admire those who tell me straight to my face if there is a problem or something on their mind. Ernie had done that and, as a result, a mutual respect has been established between us. Later in the season the fruits of the hard work Ernie and I did together were evident when Don Howe and Bobby Robson both commented in complimentary terms on the way I was turning defenders and asked if I had been practising the move. It's things like that which make all of the hard work worthwhile.

Despite the fact I had played for England and scored goals at international level during the summer, I was very much aware that the success in my first season as a Division One player with thirty-six goals to my credit would be a hard act to follow. I was beginning to get a bit concerned when I failed to score in any of the opening five games at the start of the 1985-86 season. The team had done reasonably well in winning three and drawing two matches and the irony was that when I finally got my name on the scoresheet Chelsea lost their first game of the season in a 4-1 beating at Tottenham. My overall form hadn't been too bad but it would be true to say I needed a goal to restore my full level of confidence. Being a London derby the confrontation with Spurs is always special for the Chelsea fans and contains added spice for me because Tottenham had rejected me as a youngster. I was quite pleased with the goal I scored because I was able to retain my composure when the Tottenham goalkeeper Ray Clemence left his line and lobbed the ball over him. But the team was punished severely for defensive errors and in the end we were well beaten.

It appears to be a habit of mine of getting goals in sharp bursts. Maybe it's down to confidence. I'm not really sure. Suffice to say that after the Tottenham game I embarked on a run of goalscoring which brought me success in the next couple of matches. Luton provided the next opposition which was quite a coincidence as far as I was concerned because, like Spurs, they too had rejected me as a youngster. Playing at Kenilworth Road will always be a little bit special for me. Mick Harford, who was just beginning to establish a reputation for himself as a quality striker at Luton, opened the scoring with a spectacular volley. I was determined to do my bit and the chance came when the ball broke free from a goalmouth scramble and I banged it into the net.

During the summer Luton had introduced their own version of a synthetic playing area. While the quality of their pitch is, in my opinion, far superior to the Omniturf at Queens Park Rangers I must confess I do not relish the prospect of playing on anything but grass. I can understand that small clubs unable to generate the required revenue through attendances are anxious to utilise their pitch for other activities, but the fact remains the game is just not the same. I can only hope there will not be a growth in this kind of playing surface in the Football League.

In our next match versus Southampton I was absolutely delighted to record my first goal against the great goalkeeper, Peter Shilton. I was also pleased with my performance that day because not only had I to combat Shilton but my direct opponent was Mark Wright, a centre half I rate extremely highly. It was a tragedy for Mark and England that in the FA Cup semi-finals against Liverpool later in the 1985-86 season he should break his leg in a collision with his own goalkeeper and so miss the World Cup in Mexico. I'm sure Mark is destined to become the finest centre half in England. He has got pace, height, tackles fiercely and is extremely skilful with the ball. With a bit more experience he'll take a lot of getting past. On this occasion, a long free kick from Darren Wood sailed over the heads of the entire Southampton defence. I was on to it at once, remaining very aware that Shilton is the absolute master in one against one situations. I intended to keep well away from him and, as he left his line to narrow the angle, I shot immediately and the ball flew underneath him. Shilton was magnificent after that but was eventually beaten once more by a Paul Canoville volley that gave us a 2-0 victory.

A 2-1 home win over Arsenal the following week with 33,241 supporters creating a highly-charged atmosphere at Stamford Bridge lifted Chelsea to third position in the First Division. I didn't manage to get on the scoresheet but I was particularly pleased to lay on the winning goal by going past my England colleague, Kenny Sansom, before crossing for Pat Nevin to score with a diving header. Our position in the table was not affected by a 3-1 defeat at Watford which was memorable for a fantastic goal scored by my England roommate John Barnes. He really is the most skilful of players.

David Speedie had returned against Watford after missing the two previous matches through suspension and, while Pat Nevin and I had blended well with young Kevin McAllister signed from Falkirk during the summer for just £30,000, the potency of my striking partnership with Speedie was undoubtedly feared by First Division defences. An example of this was provided in our next game against Manchester City. I got the goal which was to establish our first away success of the season after just ten minutes. Speedie began the move and after Nigel Spackman and John Bumstead had made their contribution I was in a position which left only the goalkeeper, Eric Nixon, to beat. If he had left his line positively I would have attempted to shoot past him but, as it was, he came so far and then hesitated so I gently lobbed the ball over the top of him. However, it has to be said the stars of that welcome victory were Joe McLaughlin in defence and goalkeeper Eddie Niedzwiecki. After the game the Manchester City manager, Billy McNeill, highlighted the growing reputation of my partnership with Speedie by saying: 'What a tremendous pair they are – their understanding is superb. People have criticised Dixon, but not only is he so swift to take a chance, but it's the skill he shows as well. He and Speedie move the ball so quickly. Other players need that extra touch. Not these two. Chelsea have the best duo in the business.'

It was nice to read complimentary remarks about my skills other than goalscoring but I'm not sure Mr McNeill would have been as impressed if he had seen me in action against Fourth Division Mansfield in the opening round of the Milk Cup. We had scrambled an extremely fortunate 2-2 draw in the first leg match on their ground with Pat Nevin and David Speedie rescuing our reputation after we had been two goals behind. I had a nightmare time in front of goal squandering a host of chances. Perhaps I was inspired by the remarks of the Manchester City manager in the second leg match at our own Stamford Bridge. I scored both of the goals in a 2-0 victory which gave us a 4-2 advantage on aggregate. That meant four goals in my last three matches but the tally should have been greater. In attempting to secure a hat-trick I took a penalty that was saved by the Mansfield goal-keeper Kevin Hitchcock. The new manager seemed happy enough with my contribution however. 'I was very pleased with Kerry's performance,' said John Hollins. 'He had a slow start to the season and didn't score in the first five games but he's hit a good spell now and he'll get better and better.'

The national newspapers were making much in comparing Gary Lineker and myself. Gary, who had done spectacularly well with Everton after signing for them from Leicester in a controversial £800,000 deal during the summer of 1985, was due to play at Stamford Bridge with his new team. Gary had already claimed the position as joint leading goalscorer with West Ham's Frank McAvennie. His eleven goals put him four ahead of me. But I believed comparisons between the two of us in the context of a contest for a place in the England team were not valid. In fact, the two of us had struck up a promising partnership during the summer tour.

I was very keyed up for the game which promised to be another big occasion at the Bridge against a team I admired. Chelsea and I enjoyed a dream start with a goal after just three minutes. David Speedie crossed perfectly and I was able to rise above Kevin Ratcliffe and Pat Van Den Hauwe to beat goalkeeper Neville Southall with a header. Chelsea proceeded to play some great stuff against the reigning League Champions. The Everton goalkeeper was booked for protesting at the awarding of a penalty to us after he was judged to have tripped David Speedie. Later in the game he was sensationally sent off following a second bookable offence when he handled the ball outside his penalty area to prevent me racing through unopposed. Ironically, Nigel Spackman became the latest Chelsea player to miss with the spot-kick, though our spirits were revived by a great goal from Speedie near half-time. Before the referee had time to signal the end of the opening forty-five minutes Everton's Kevin Sheedy pulled a goal back. It was certainly a thrilling game for the supporters and although Everton demonstrated their undoubted class with some fierce resistance after being reduced to ten men Chelsea captured the points.

Oxford United, newly promoted to the First Division and managed by Maurice Evans, the man who had brought me into professional football, were next in line. Oxford were to fight a successful battle against relegation throughout the season and they certainly had the beating of Chelsea as far as the First Division was concerned. I managed to get my name among the goalscorers again but Oxford won the match through a truly spectacular goal from the ex-Chelsea player Peter Rhoades-Brown. This setback didn't disturb Chelsea's third position but the real test of our League Championship potential was to be provided on 26th October with the visit to Stamford Bridge of Manchester United. Ron Atkinson's team was currently racing away with the First Division and winning match after match. Extra spice was provided by intense newspaper speculation about United's desire to buy me from Chelsea. The story went that the United and former Arsenal centre forward, Frank Stapleton, would be used in a part-exchange deal. The situation disturbed me because I confess there had been times when I had begun to doubt whether the new manager really rated me as a player. There were several rumours floating around suggesting that Hollins was not entirely sold on my abilities. I decided the only way to discover whether there was any substance to these rumours was to seek a heart-to-heart talk with Hollins who assured me there was not a grain of truth in the newspaper stories. His words obviously eased my mind considerably. Later in that same season the chairman made a point of pre-empting further newspaper speculation about a transfer to Manchester United by revealing he had received a firm inquiry from the Old Trafford chairman, Martin Edwards. At the time, United had agreed to sell Mark Hughes to Barcelona for £2 million but Mr Bates insisted he would want £5 million for me. I was extremely flattered by both the interest of United and the reaction of the chairman but remained disturbed at the doubts which had been sown in my mind about whether the manager valued fully my contribution.

There were 42,485 in attendance at Stamford Bridge for the Manchester United game. Jesper Olsen, the Danish international, put United ahead but Joe McLaughlin levelled the scores after a hectic scramble in the United penalty area. For one glorious moment I thought I had put us in front when I caught the ball perfectly on the run with my right foot. Gary Bailey, in the United goal, was beaten all the way but the ball cannoned off the underside of the crossbar to safety. As in the previous home game against Everton we were faced with having to play against ten men when United's Graeme Hogg was sent off for a second bookable offence. It's a strange phenomenon in football that so often it can be more difficult to break down ten men than eleven. United organised themselves well and fought magnificently. Mark Hughes demonstrated superbly why Barcelona were tempted to invest £2 million in his talent later that season by turning in an instant on the edge of our penalty area before smacking an unstoppable shot beyond goalkeeper Eddie Niedzwiecki. Hughes is not a prolific goalscorer but the ones he gets tend to be brilliantly spectacular. This goal won United the match, though we believed we had in no way deserved to lose.

The result meant that United had strengthened their position at the top while Chelsea dropped down to fifth. We were to experience a double fright in the next round of the Milk Cup as well. After earning a draw at Stamford Bridge against near neighbours Fulham we just managed to scrape through against the Second Division team in the replay. I scored the winning goal but once again the hero of the hour was goalkeeper Niedzwiecki. He survived a barrage of Fulham attacks making unbelievable point-blank saves. It was without doubt the greatest exhibition of goalkeeping I have ever witnessed. It was performances like these which deservedly won for Eddie the Player of the Year award at Chelsea. The honour was made even more remarkable by the fact that Eddie was to sustain a bad knee injury during a game at QPR in March and was unable to play in any more matches during the 1985-86 season.

Following the defeat by United our league form re-established itself with four straight victories. The first was at Ipswich and brought a goal which was acclaimed in many quarters as the finest of my career. It came in only the second minute of the game at Portman Road. Young Robert Isaac crossed from the right, David Speedie flicked the ball on and Pat Nevin headed it back across the penalty area. I didn't hesitate in volleying the ball perfectly from fifteen yards. The Ipswich goalkeeper, Paul Cooper, said later: 'I've been in the First Division for eleven years and that was as good a goal as I have had scored against me.' Terry Butcher, the first choice England centre half, was sitting in the stands because he had not recovered fully from a knee operation. He commented: 'It was a quality goal from a quality player.' Remarks like these, especially from fellow professionals, are exceptionally pleasing. I received almost as much pleasure from setting up my partner

Speedie for the second goal after eleven minutes as I had from my own effort. I dispossessed a defender before pulling the ball back across the face of goal for David to run in and score. Yet, once again, while Speedie and I had made our contributions with goals we had reason to be grateful to our goalkeeper who produced stunning saves to protect the advantage we had established.

On the morning of the home game against Nottingham Forest the following week, the newspapers made it clear that I would be awarded my home debut for England in the World Cup qualifying game against Northern Ireland if I was to stay clear of injury. I knew I could not afford to take anything for granted and was determined to demonstrate my goalscoring abilities in front of Bobby Robson who was scheduled to attend the match.

It turned out to be a marvellously entertaining game, later described as a tribute to all that is best in English Football. I was able to celebrate a couple of goals as was Nigel Clough. It was the first time I had seen the son of the famous Forest manager in action and any suspicions that a touch of nepotism might be involved in his selection was instantly dispelled. I saw enough on the one occasion to believe we'll hear a lot more about young Nigel Clough in the future. He is a sound, skilful player with a neat first touch. He passes the ball firmly and accurately and when his opportunities came to score he was calm and clinical about it. David Speedie had put Chelsea in front after just two minutes and Clough equalised four minutes later. In the 25th minute I was able to spring Forest's offside trap with a burst of pace and lift the ball passed goalkeeper Steve Sutton. Before half-time we had a third goal: Mickey Hazzard, signed from Spurs for £300,000, evaded the familiar Chelsea trap of missed penalties and made no mistake after Forest's Garry Birtles had handled. Clough pulled one back but I was able to confirm that Forest's run of seven successive victories had come to a close by scoring our fourth goal. It was my thirteenth goal of the season so far and I was extremely happy with my game.

There was criticism, covered elsewhere in the book, of my play in my Wembley debut against Northern Ireland on the

Wednesday and when we arrived at Newcastle for the Saturday game I was treated to the usual kind of stick by the Geordie fans. Chelsea hadn't won at St James Park for fourteen years and Newcastle were a team with a growing reputation. We were a goal behind after just seventy seconds through a superb diving header from Glenn Roeder. But David Speedie produced an equaliser shortly before the interval. A half-time roasting from John Hollins ensured it was a more positive performance from Chelsea in the second half. I'd come close to putting us ahead on a couple of occasions and with twelve minutes remaining one of my goal attempts was fumbled by goalkeeper Martin Thomas and Nigel Spackman followed up to score. In the 82nd minute Nigel produced a great run and cross for me to score easily from close range. The occasion was my one hundredth League game for Chelsea and my 62nd goal in those games. The team had regained third place in the First Division and it was a contented band of players who made the long journey home on that Saturday night.

Home victory over Aston Villa and another goal for me kept up the pressure in the higher reaches of the First Division. All of the players and staff at Chelsea also had high hopes of success in the cup competitions. We had a tough draw in the Milk Cup – albeit at home – with a tie against Everton. It was a big night a Stamford Bridge and we couldn't have got off to a better start when I scored from close range within a minute. But Everton equalised within two minutes with a free kick from Kevin Sheedy. A slip by our captain Colin Pates made it an unlucky thirteenth minute for us and Paul Bracewell put Everton in front. Just as in our First Division game earlier in the season, Everton had a player sent off when a disputed free kick brought such a welter of protest from Sheedy that referee Dennis Hedges not only booked him but dismissed him from the field. Once again Everton organised themselves splendidly and, although I was able to create the chance from which Pat Nevin equalised five minutes before half-time, we were unable to overcome their ten men and a replay at Goodison Park was inevitable.

Before that we had to travel north to play the mighty Liverpool at Anfield in a First Division match. David Speedie had been allowed to travel with Scotland for their vital World Cup qualifying game in Australia and injuries sustained in the tough tie against Everton meant that we were far from at full strength. Jerry Murphy, another summer signing, came into the team along with Keith Jones who in my opinion is a young player with a fine future. He works hard in training and has an eye for goals. He played well at Liverpool that day in a fine all-round performance from Chelsea. We were denied a blatant penalty in the opening half when Pat Nevin was brought down by Steve Nicol as he was about to score and, to add insult to injury, when Ian Rush tumbled in our area with just four minutes remaining, Liverpool were allowed to take the lead through a Jan Molby spot-kick. Our centre half Joe McLaughlin swears to this day he made no contact with Rush whatsoever. So, what had been a brave, fighting, performance from a depleted team seemed certain to be unrewarded until Pat Nevin popped up to beat the Liverpool goalkeeper Bruce Grobbelaar after a goalmouth scramble. In a thrilling finish we almost snatched the victory we thought we deserved but the effort was cleared off the Liverpool goal-line.

At this time, the first ever Full Members Cup competition was in full swing and after victories over Portsmouth, Charlton and West Brom we needed to overcome Oxford United over two legs to win the Southern Area final and qualify to play the Northern Area winners in a match we hoped would be staged at Wembley. In the first leg at Oxford we were reduced to ten men after twenty-seven minutes when Keith Jones was sent off for a clumsy challenge on Peter Rhoades-Brown. Yet, we succeeded in taking the lead after thirty-three minutes when the Oxford defender Neil Slatter turned a cross of mine into his own net. Four minutes into the second half a great through pass from Pat Nevin set me off on a run in which I outpaced a defender, dummied the goalkeeper and scored. John Aldridge, another natural goalscorer for whom I have the utmost regard, pulled one back from a penalty but I was able to collect another couple of goals before the end to establish a marvellous 4-1 victory.

This was my first hat-trick of the 1985-86 season and the eighth of my career. My old friend Maurice Evans was gracious enough even in defeat, to comment: 'He's the best striker in the country. They say he can't do this and can't do that – but he just keeps on scoring goals.' Typical Maurice. A nice, decent, honest man whether in victory or defeat. I was absolutely delighted for him when Oxford went on to win the Milk Cup at Wembley that season. The joy of our triumph at Oxford was enhanced by a public declaration of intent from our chairman Ken Bates. He had told me before the game that if we were to win the Southern Area Final he would underwrite the guarantees necessary to persuade the Wembley Stadium authorities to stage the national final. I was delighted because I dearly wanted to witness my Chelsea team-mates experiencing the kind of thrill I had enjoyed by appearing at Wembley. Unknown to me at the time was the fact that injury would keep me out of the big day. But almost 70,000 people were at Wembley to vindicate the marvellous efforts of our chairman and the chief of Manchester City, Peter Swales.

Following a drab, disappointing First Division game at Coventry in which a goal from Jerry Murphy gave us a point, we were due to make the trek north for the important Milk Cup fourth round replay against Everton. A few days previously, I had travelled to Paris along with the Everton manager Howard Kendall to collect my Golden Boot Award for being the joint top scorer with Gary Lineker the previous season. Mr Kendall was collecting Europe's Team of the Year Award for Everton, as well as representing Gary who was suffering from a groin strain. I liked the Everton manager immediately. He seemed to me to be an open, engaging, friendly man with a deep knowledge of the game. Before we parted on our return journey he jokingly remarked: 'Take it easy in the replay. We can do without those early goals of yours.'

I couldn't help but recall those words on the night of the replay at Goodison Park. A long ball from David Speedie allowed me to race past my England colleague Gary Stevens before clipping a shot in off the far post. The official time of that goal was just sixty-one seconds. I never did discover Mr Kendall's thoughts at that moment! Gary Lineker, having recovered from his injury problems, was showing remarkable goalscoring form and he produced his sixteenth strike of that season to equalise. But with just fifteen minutes remaining our big centre back Joe McLaughlin moved forward for a corner and drove home the winner. It was a remarkable victory and thoroughly deserved.

Five successive victories in the First Division followed establishing Chelsea as a team to be feared. And yet strangely I was able to score on only one occasion. We'd beaten Sheffield Wednesday and Birmingham when the time came to meet Spurs and Luton once again in successive matches. A big crowd of 37,115 was at the Bridge for the Tottenham game on 28th December. I came close to scoring on a couple of occasions before finally getting a header passed Ray Clemence in the nineteenth minute. I hit the post later in the game and Nigel Spackman wrapped up the points with a successful penalty. The victory was enough to carry Chelsea into second position in the League, just two points behind Manchester United. Victories over Luton and West Bromwich Albion maintained our momentum.

Everything seemed set fair for a successful season for Chelsea and Kerry Dixon. I had proved for the second successive season that I could and would score goals at the highest levels and the club was positioned perfectly for a sustained challenge not only in the League Championship but also in the Milk Cup and FA Cup. Little did I suspect that one horrific moment was about to wreck my own season and seriously damage Chelsea's hopes of at least one major honour.

A goal from Pat Nevin had provided a most satisfying draw in the Milk Cup fifth round against Queens Park Rangers with the replay to come at our own Stamford Bridge. We'd reached the fourth round of the FA Cup by virtue of a lone goal from David Speedie which had accounted for Second Division Shrewsbury.

On Sunday, 26th January Liverpool would provide the FA Cup opposition in a game which was to be televised live. Understandably, we strongly fancied our chances of winning. After all we had won all of the honours if not the three points with a depleted team only a short while before at Anfield. I was psyched up for the game and believed my pace could cause problems for Alan Hansen and Mark Lawrenson at the centre of the Liverpool defence. Alas, I was not to get the opportunity to put the theory to the test. A mere six minutes had elapsed when I was called upon to contest a high ball with the Liverpool defenders. I took off from the left foot and, just as I twisted in mid-air to attain the extra lift required, I felt an excruciating pain in my stomach. I killed the jump immediately and slumped down onto the floor. I knew straight away I was hurt and hurt badly. I couldn't move my legs at all. I raised my arm to signal my distress to the bench, was carried off the field on a stretcher and into the dressing room. The club doctor decided I was in too much pain to attempt an immediate examination and advised me to take a bath, saying he would check me later. But I couldn't move at all let alone drag myself over to the team bath. I was unable to raise even my head and shoulders and although I kept on trying and trying there was no response, only an agonising ache in my stomach. Mum, Dad and my business manager Brian Roach, realising that something was seriously wrong, came down to the dressing room. I couldn't tell them what the problem was because I didn't know myself. An ambulance was called and arrived shortly after half-time. As I was leaving Stamford Bridge I heard that David Speedie had scored a magnificent goal but Liverpool were leading 2-1. All the way to the hospital I prayed that somehow Chelsea would snatch an equaliser. At that stage I was convinced I would be fit to play in any replay. Little did I know just how wrong I could be.

At the hospital doctors hastily carried out tests for a hernia or a rupture and, in the end, detected a torn stomach muscle which had encroached into the groin area, affecting the whole of my left side. The news that Chelsea had been beaten in the game depressed me even more. I was detained overnight in hospital for observation and slowly the realisation hit me that I was going to be out of action for a considerable period of time. The hospital prognosis was that I would be unable to play for a month and that I would probably be on the sidelines for a much longer period.

I managed to limp along to the vital Milk Cup replay against QPR on the following Wednesday to lend what little support I could to the lads. A 2-0 defeat meant we had been knocked out of both of the major cup competitions in the space of just three days. The wintry weather conditions ensured that I was to miss just two League games because of the injury – a home draw against Leicester and a shock 4-1 home defeat by Oxford. In fact, after intensive treatment to the injury every morning and afternoon I was able to make an ill-fated return to action in the England international game against Israel in Tel-Aviv. My first game for Chelsea was at home to Manchester City on 8th March and, although we achieved a victory through a solitary goal, I was far from satisfied that I had been restored to full fitness.

I was indebted to John Hollins for his patience and understanding in what was a traumatic period in my professional career. Physically the injury was not a problem but mentally I was haunted by the fear that the stomach muscle would tear again. I am sure that in the initial period of my return to football I was a yard slower off the mark because of this subconscious concern. The manager was superb. He resisted the temptation to play me in reserve team matches insisting that what I needed was First Division football to restore the sharpness in my play. Don't forget that Chelsea retained an active interest in the League Championship campaign and could ill-afford to carry any player who was not one hundred per cent fit.

I'm sure that if I could have got myself on the scoresheet in the next couple of games it would have worked wonders for my confidence. But the fixtures against Everton at Goodison Park and Queens Park Rangers at home produced 1-1 draws with goals for Jerry Murphy and Pat Nevin respectively. My contribution was, in truth, pretty anonymous. The misery increased, despite a 1-0 victory at Southampton with a winner from our captain Colin Pates. The following day we were scheduled to meet Manchester City in the Members Cup Final with the venue of Wembley Stadium as promised by our chairman. I had been withdrawn from the England squad to play in Russia on the following Wednesday because of the game. I sustained a slight groin injury at Southampton, which was in no way connected with the previous complaint. The newspapers put two and two together and came up with five. Speculation was rife that I was struggling to make a comeback and that since my return I had looked nothing like the real Kerry Dixon. That part, at least, bore some resemblance to the truth. I knew in my own mind I wasn't the same player. Even so, no professional passes up an opportunity to play at Wembley without a fight. I underwent a fitness test on the Wembley pitch an hour before the kick-off against Manchester City and at the end of it the manager and I decided together it would be best not to risk incurring further damage.

The game was, without question, the biggest day in Chelsea's season. The occasion provided a marvellous match with my striking partner David Speedie hitting a hat-trick and Colin Lee making the most of his opportunity in replacing me to score a couple himself. Manchester City launched a remarkable comeback in the later stages of the game and the scoreline ended up 5-4 in Chelsea's favour. The game had presented the finest possible advertisement for football in England. Wembley had expected a sparse attendance but a crowd of almost 70,000 assembled and their behaviour was exemplary. I was delighted for my teammates who had worked hard and deserved some success in the 1985-86 season. However, it's not easy to feel part of the picture when you have not played in the game and I had suffered a double blow: I had missed out on both a Wembley appearance and the opportunity of another England cap. It was certainly no comfort to learn that Mark Hateley was also troubled by injury and unable to play for England against Russia in Tblisi. In the event, the repercussions of missing that international were to be felt with devastating effect when the World Cup got underway in the summer of 1986. Gary Lineker and Peter Beardsley performed well as an alternative strike force and when England manager Bobby Robson decided in Mexico that changes in attack must be made, he opted for that combination rather than bring me into the team in place of Hateley.

It was a thoroughly miserable time for me and the agony was far from over. Chelsea remained fourth in the League and a local derby game against West Ham on 29th March was likely to answer pertinent questions about the title campaign. The Hammers, too, had enjoyed a marvellous season and harboured genuine ambitions of their first ever League Championship triumph. The build-up to the confrontation between the two London clubs commanded acres of space in the national press. The pundits were having a field day. It was suggested quite forcibly that because of my halting recovery and the success of Colin Lee in my place at Wembley that the manager should stick with the same team. Rumours abounded that I was unhappy at Chelsea because secretly the manager didn't rate me. Once again I began to wonder if these stories had been fired by someone within the club. Seldom are such rumours printed without a grain of truth behind them.

Although I had been unable to do any training during that week I was fit enough to join in the Good Friday session before the vital game against West Ham. We also had an equally important meeting on Easter Monday with QPR. I declared myself fit to play to John Hollins but when he eventually named the team to play the Hammers I was not included. I went along to see him and asked him why. He replied that because I had been unfit to train for most of the week he couldn't see any point in rushing me back into the team for one game and risk a breakdown when he would need me for many more games before the end of the season. I could understand the logic of his argument especially when he assured me that I would be in the team no matter what against QPR on the Monday, after further training sessions over the weekend. Later friends advised me against playing at QPR reasoning that if I was not fit enough to play on the Saturday I would be risking further damage by turning out on the Monday. I preferred to listen to the manager. What he had said to me made sound sense. I was determined to concentrate on playing against Rangers.

Colin Lee took my place in the team once more in the home game against West Ham. The Hammers were magnificent that day, playing some glorious attacking football and beating Chelsea 4-0. There would have been nothing Kerry Dixon could have done about it. I was flabbergasted, however, to receive telephone calls that night from Sunday newspaper journalists asking for my comments on a statement from the manager which said I had been fit to play against West Ham but simply not selected. I chose to say nothing. The following morning the papers were full of the story. I was confused, I was angry, I was depressed all at the same time. The manager had told me I was being rested because he wanted me in the team to play against QPR on the Monday. I just couldn't understand why he didn't appear to be saying the same thing to the press.

That morning I went down to the ground where I found Ernie Walley and had a long chat with him. I told him straight out what was on my mind. From where I was standing it looked as though Chelsea wanted me out of the team. Ernie went into the manager's office to telephone John Hollins at home and after a brief chat he put me on the telephone. The manager insisted he had not been quoted accurately by the newspapers. He explained he had allowed the press to interpret the situation as they saw fit and said I should understand the kind of tricks newspaper reporters were capable of getting up to because I had suffered myself in the past. He assured me once more I would be in the team on the Monday. I accepted what he had to say. I wasn't looking for a row, but I must confess I remained disturbed by the entire business.

Easter Monday 1986 at Loftus Road is not a day I will forget in a hurry. We were beaten 6-0. Rangers seemed to score every time they attacked while we couldn't muster a decent shot all afternoon. A draw against Ipswich followed and my confidence, badly in need of the boost a goal would bring, would have to wait another four days. That was when we were due to meet Manchester United at Old Trafford. They had suffered a terrible run and the awesome lead they had established at the top of the First Division earlier in the season had been eroded. They desperately needed to beat Chelsea to revive any chance of taking the title.

On paper we looked easy meat. United attacked relentlessly

during the first half in front of their home crowd of 45,355. The doubts about my true fitness remained and I was very much aware that my chances of going to the World Cup finals with England were diminishing rapidly. At the beginning of the second half I took a pass in the centre circle and was off down the middle. The adrenalin flowed. I felt sure, I felt confident, using my pace to hold off the United defenders who were desperately scurrying back to cover. The killer instinct returned. I looked up, measured the distance that goalkeeper Chris Turner had covered off his line and slipped the ball beyond him. Some people have said it was the best goal I have ever scored. I don't know about that but boy was it welcome. With just a few minutes remaining David Speedie made a great run down the right and crossed perfectly. The old predatory instinct took over again and I swept the ball first time into the net. I'd never scored against Manchester United before and the rumours about them maintaining an interest in signing me added a touch of piquancy to the situation. I felt sorry for Manchester United and their manager Ron Atkinson. They had led the League for so long and played with such style. Our victory had ended all hopes they had harboured of a first League Championship since 1967. I confess I was elated for myself. I had emerged from a long, dark and lonely tunnel. Later that night the goals were shown on television. To this day, I believe their execution confirmed my place in the England squad for the World Cup.

For an all too brief time our own championship aspirations flared again but a goalless draw against Forest in an appalling game hardly helped matters. The crunch, we thought, would come in a visit to Upton Park for another confrontation with West Ham. I was convinced that Bobby Robson would be there to make a final assessment of my form before naming his World Cup squad. In the event, his assistant Don Howe was at the game. I was unable to score a goal myself but did succeed in turning Alvin Martin in the penalty area before crossing for Pat Nevin to head our winner in a 2-1 victory. We had lifted ourselves into third position but unfortunately our hopes were swamped by some poor play in our remaining five matches.

In the next game we could manage only a 1-1 draw at home to Newcastle and proceeded to tumble to a 3-1 defeat at Aston Villa. A further setback occurred at Highbury when goals from Viv Anderson and Charlie Nicholas condemned us to another defeat. When Liverpool arrived at Stamford Bridge on Saturday, 3rd May we were well adrift, while the Anfield team required victory to clinch the title for themselves. Kenny Dalglish, in his first season as a player-manager, could not have written a more romantic script for himself. Dalglish, a superb player and masterly finisher, claimed the winner with a classic example of goalscoring. He ran into our penalty area, controlled the ball on his chest and then volleyed it into the far corner of the net before it had hit the ground. Liverpool proceeded to collect the League Championship and FA Cup double with a brilliant victory over neighbours Everton in the first-ever all Merseyside final at Wembley.

However, there was to be no happy ending to the 1985-86 season for Kerry Dixon. In fact, it culminated in a heated row with manager John Hollins. Our last First Division game of the season was at Watford just twenty-four hours before I was due to join the England squad departing for the World Cup. On the night before the game I received a telephone call from my business manager Brian Roach advising me of a major story which would appear in the *Daily Mirror* the following morning. According to Brian the big bold headline would proclaim: 'Dixon Axed' and he had been assured by a *Mirror* reporter that the story was one hundred per cent accurate. Chelsea had recently signed a new striker, Gordon Durie, from the Scottish club Hibernians for £400,000, and I knew the club was anxious to try him out before the end of the season. To be honest, I paid little heed to the warning that the story was about to appear, but lo and behold, there it was the following day.

I joined up with the team at the appointed time the next day and following our pre-match meal I was pulled me to one side by the manager. The kick-off was just ninety minutes away. Mr Hollins said that because I was going off to the World Cup he intended to leave me out so he could try a couple of new tactics. I told him, in no uncertain terms, that World Cup or not I wanted to play in the game. However, he was insistent that he wished to see the new boy in the team in a system which employed two wingers in Paul Canoville and Kevin McAllister, meaning there was no room for Pat Nevin either. Once again I was angry, disappointed and dismayed all at the same time. Harsh words were exchanged between us although, at the end of the day, I had no alternative but to accede to his wishes. When I questioned how it should be that the press were aware of exactly what was going to occur in the team selection he insisted they had merely been guessing. In that case they had guessed exactly right, I retorted, and left the room.

It was clear that I had a lot of hard thinking to do during the summer while I was away with the England squad. As soon as the World Cup was over it would be necessary to seek another meeting with the manager.

KERRY

People have often asked me about my unusual name. It was, in fact, Mum's idea and she stuck to it despite some formidable opposition from Dad. I'm told I didn't like it too much when I was a kid and announced to the family I intended to change it to Michael when I got older. Thank goodness I didn't. As the name is slightly different it is, therefore, distinctive and over the years it has proved to be a great asset in grabbing the headlines. An obvious advantage is that I don't think there is another professional footballer of the same name.

Mum tells me she first heard the name when watching an Australian athlete running in a steeplechase race. He fell at one of the hurdles and whether she felt sorry for him or not I don't know, but the name Kerry O'Brien stuck in her mind. Later, she was returning by train from London with my Dad and there was a lad in the compartment whose name was Kerry. It was then she pronounced that if the baby she was carrying was a boy she intended to call him Kerry. Dad wasn't so keen and warned I wouldn't like it when I grew up. I am comfortable with the name now and rather like it. If the letters from members of my fan club are anything to go by then the name is becoming much more popular as many people have written to say they intend to call their child Kerry.

I have always been able to enjoy and relish a close-knit relationship with my family. My sister Jane has provided assistance even in the establishment of my football career. She was a bit of a tomboy in her younger days and was always willing to play the goalkeeper if I wanted to practise my shooting. When I was working in the engineering factory Dad would get me out of bed at six o'clock in the morning to report for practice in a field at the back of the house. It is those kind of memories which I treasure. Without the assistance of my family the chances are I would not have become a successful footballer. They have also prevented me from playing the big star even if I wanted to. The fact I spend a great deal of time at home with my parents means my feet are fixed firmly on the ground. I've no doubt that Mum would still give me a clip around the ear if she suspected I was getting above myself. Luckily I don't believe my character has changed, or should I say been allowed to change. The bright lights of London do not appeal as I've seen for myself the effect the trendy nightclubs and watering holes can have on the career of a promising footballer. I have my own mates back in Luton who appreciate me as Kerry Dixon the bloke rather than Kerry Dixon the footballer and I have always been careful to guard against attracting the hangers-on who tend to attach themselves like limpets to anyone in the public eye.

My one great passion in life – obsession if you like – is goalscoring. As far as I am concerned there is no other feeling quite like it. It's impossible to put into words exactly how I feel when I put the ball in the net and it feels just the same same whether in street games as a kid or in the Aztec Stadium in Mexico during the summer of 1985. Most people would expect that players who don't score goals regularly experience a greater sensation of achievement than those for whom it is an everyday occurrence. But that's not true. I am elated by even the simplest of tap-ins. I suppose a goalkeeper enjoys a similar sensation when he pulls off a great save or stops a penalty.

After Chelsea had confirmed promotion back to the First Division I moved into a house of my own for a short while. I was forever getting kids knocking at the front door asking for my autograph and one day they called and asked if I would sponsor them for the number of goals they would score in a cup final which was to be played on Luton Town's ground. When they called again to collect the money after a 1-1 draw they asked if I would consider coaching them the following season. I was impressed by their politeness and agreed, not knowing for a moment what it would entail. To be honest I had forgotten all about it when a knock came on my door again the following August. Chelsea had already completed a couple of First Division games and the kids' team-manager had called round to inform me their season began on the following Sunday. I went to watch them play in their first friendly game and was pleasantly surprised. They won 3-0 and I arranged a couple of training sessions with them. Bramingham Spitfires will not mean anything to people outside the small vicinity within Luton but those lads have provided me with so much pleasure. The manager is a chap called Doug Roe and his wife Jan is the club secretary. I just couldn't help but get involved because they were such nice people.

Obviously, the main guidance I give to the boys is in how to score goals. Many books have been written on the subject but in truth there can be no hard and fast rules. Goalscorers are born not made. But there are some basic guidelines to be followed. I have always tried to concentrate on getting the ball on target at least. My Dad always advised that if in doubt shoot straight for the goalkeeper since the philosophy is that on many occasions you will not be totally accurate so, as long as the ball has been kept low, there will always be an excellent chance of scoring. Even it the goalkeeper makes a save there is always the possibility of a rebound. It's amazing the number of times this tactic can be successful. I tell my Bramingham boys to be totally single-minded about scoring goals. It's important never to be afraid to miss a chance and even if you have scored one goal, start looking for the next immediately. These are two of my greatest strengths. I can remember once having squandered four decent goalscoring opportunities. Some players might not have wanted to suffer the embarrassment of missing any more but I reasoned that if I got another couple of chances and scored from both I would have a return of two goals from six chances, which is a decent ratio in anybody's book. I ended up scoring the two goals and the lesson stuck with me.

Players, managers, coaches and the public can talk about the art of goalscoring until they are blue in the face but the true goalscorer possesses an intangible sixth sense which gets him into the correct position to put the ball in the net. Of course, the goalscorer will have assets apparent to the eye: he may be quick, he may be great in the air, he may have an explosive shot. All of these qualities are bound to be of assistance, but attempting to tell people how to score goals is like a football pools winner explaining how he did it – most of the time it's pure instinct.

I class strikers in two totally different catagories. It's not just a question of being a big or a little man either. For example, David Speedie at Chelsea is a good striker. He twists, turns, competes, possesses a prodigious leap for a little man and has a good shot, he's a highly rated striker and deservedly so. I am an out and out goalscorer. My record shows I can and will get goals from every conceivable position. Last season David matched me almost goal for goal at Chelsea but you would not have got a bet against me finishing leading goalscorer at the end of the season. It's when a manager can combine a striker like Speedie and a goalscorer like myself that he has a winning partnership.

Mark Hughes, sold by Manchester United to Barcelona for £2 million at the end of the 1985-86 season, is a fine striker with good control who can hold up the play, shield the ball and bring his colleagues into play, but he's not a goalscorer. His partner in that year at Old Trafford was Frank Stapleton, another fine player but he, too, is not a natural goalscorer. It could be argued that United lost their chance of clinching the League Championship in that season after surrendering what had appeared to be an unassailable lead at the top because their strikers didn't score enough goals. Goals win matches. It's as simple as that. I am the first to admit I do not possess the outstanding skills on the ball of someone like Glenn Hoddle and I'll never be a Diego Maradona but I have other assets which many consider equally important.

I can remember watching Malcolm Macdonald play for Luton when I was just a kid, standing on the terraces and being amazed by his electrifying pace, lethal shot and considerable heading ability. The supporters loved him. He excited them. He once scored all five goals for England in an international match against Cyprus but still his critics insisted he couldn't play. What nonsense. There are so many varying aspects to the game of football and it is not without significance that goalscorers are the most highly-priced commodity in the professional game. I have worked tremendously hard at improving my own touch and technique, and although I think it is very important to work hard at your shortcomings, it is much more vital to work at what you are good at. If I thought for one moment that by concentrating on becoming a more complete player the goalscoring would suffer I would have no hesitation whatsoever in sticking to what I am good at. My pace and physique are obvious assets in my play. I also relish a challenge and perhaps that's why I have a good record against the best central defensive partnerships. Mark Lawrenson and Alan Hansen at Liverpool are excellent defenders but they are far from comfortable when the ball is knocked in behind them and they are forced to deal with my speed off the mark. Everton's Kevin Ratcliffe and Derek Mountfield harbour similar fears and I've got my share of goals against them.

Ian Rush, of Liverpool and Wales, is, in my opinion, the finest all-round striker in the game. He is a great goalscorer and has the ability to hold up the ball and bring his colleagues into play. He is complete. Yet, the critics persist in seeking out a weakness in his game. Ah, they say, but he cannot head a ball. I have seen Rushy score some superb goals with his head. What they will come up with next I just don't know.

I was made aware of the value in being a goalscorer at an early age when I was still at Challney School, after a few of us were caught playing cards by a schoolmaster. We were told to report to Mr Howells who was the sportsmaster and I was the last in line outside his office. A lad called Eddie Woods, still a close pal of mine, was called in first and within minutes the word had passed along the queue that he had been suspended from school. A similar fate befell everyone else in front of me when it was my turn to be confronted by the irate Mr Howells. 'I'm very surprised at you, Dixon,' said Mr Howells. 'You are the last boy I would have expected to be involved in something like this.' He told me he intended to telephone my home and insisted I informed my Dad what had occurred before he made the call. I was dreading it. I returned home and duly informed Dad what had happened. He was grim-faced but said nothing. After a lengthy telephone conversation with Mr Howells, he told me that I was to report to the sportsmaster the following morning. The next day Mr Howells told me he had considered a caning or a period of suspension, similar to the punishment inflicted on the other boys in the class, but had decided against it because it would mean me missing the cup final that the school team was involved in. He told me to rejoin my class and to be sure to score a hat-trick. We won the match 6-3, I scored three goals, this being the first time I came to realise the importance of being a good goalscorer!

Since my professional debut I believe I have improved considerably as an all-round player but it remains the goals I score which provide my notoriety. I have scored them with Reading, Chelsea and England, yet every step of the way it seems I have still had to prove myself. So much of the art of goalscoring is based on confidence, and statistics show that at some stage in every season a striker will have a run when it seems he just cannot score. It's also said that statistics show most players will score one goal from every four chances. I'd like to believe my ratio is one in three and the number of goals I have recorded in my career would suggest I remain close to the mark.

As far as I am concerned there is no such thing as a bad goal; so long as the ball beats the goalkeeper and crosses the goal-line I am happy. I have scored a few spectacular goals in my time, but many more tap-ins and close range side-footers. I think the best goal I have ever scored was at Old Trafford towards the end of the 1985-86 season. Manchester United were striving to win the Championship and had put us under extreme pressure throughout the opening half. I was still not a hundred per cent fit following a bad injury but, within a minute of the restart, Mike Hazzard put me in the clear. I had to run with the ball from just inside United's half of the field with their central defenders, Paul McGrath and Mark Higgins in hot pursuit. Their goalkeeper, Chris Turner, advanced but held his ground. So often a goalkeeper will make it easier for a forward by rushing out and flinging himself recklessly at the striker's feet. Then it is a simple task of slipping the ball either under him or over his body. But Turner held firm. The defenders were closing in rapidly as I moved to go to my left and then slipped the ball the other way beyond the goalkeeper. I was so pleased because they are the hardest goals of all to score when you have had to run a long way with plenty of time for thought. In the last few minutes of the game I scored the winner, sweeping in a pass from David Speedie. In comparison to the first goal that was a simple task because I had no time to think about what I was going to do. The shot was purely instinctive.

Scoring goals like that, even in such a daunting environment as a packed Old Trafford, is no different a task than at either Dunstable or Reading. Of course, the stakes are higher but the single-minded objective is entirely the same. Nor does it follow necessarily that having scored thirty-six goals during a season in the First Division a player could expect to return to somewhere like the Third Division and score an equal amount or even more. There is a widely held belief that because a striker is backed up by superior players in the First Division he should become a better goalscorer. I cannot adhere to this theory simply because in the higher divisions the quality of defenders and goalkeepers is also greater.

Strikers will always have a much better chance if they study their opposing goalkeepers, so many of whom make it easy to put goals passed them because they commit themselves recklessly under pressure. Such accusations can never be levelled against Peter Shilton. His very presence can undermine the confidence of even the most accomplished goalscorer. When I am involved with England it is always a comforting sight to see Shilton in goal, but when it comes to playing against his club, Southampton, the sheer physical form of the man makes for a daunting sight. He is the best goalkeeper I have ever come across in a one against one situation. He forces the striker to commit himself rather than the other way around, pitting his own confidence and nerve against the opposition. He stands firm, crouched low, ready to spring in any direction and his agility for man of his size is incredible.

I can recall a situation during an England practice session in the Aztec Stadium when the ball came to me and I believed I had been presented with a simple tap-in. But Shilton somehow got across and stopped the shot. I couldn't believe it. I'd thought it would have been impossible for him to intervene and it proved to me that it's not sensible to take any kind of liberties with a goalkeeper like Shilton. At a competitive level I have managed to score just one goal passed him in four meetings before the end of the 1985-86 season. The game was at Stamford Bridge and we beat Southampton 2-0, my opportunity arriving when I volleyed the ball first time and beat his dive. Neville Southall is another goalkeeper I admire tremendously although my goalscoring record against him and Everton is not at all bad. He, too, presents a massive physical barrier to any striker with goals on his mind.

From the moment I became a full-time professional footballer my attitude to life changed dramatically. The couldn't-care-less attitude had to go as there is no doubt in my mind now that my own immature attitude to life in my teenage years played a major part in the heart-breaking rejections by both Luton and Tottenham. However, I have fought back and can state in all honesty that I believe I am as dedicated to my profession as any other player in the game. I am proud of my record as a goalscorer. I am working hard to become a more complete all-round centre forward and have tried to accept criticism in the right spirit and to make constructive use of it.

Throughout my career I have never lost sight of the need to prove myself time and time again. There were doubts about me succeeding with Reading after the rejections by Luton and Tottenham, followed by yet more when I moved into the Second

Division with Chelsea. Then it was can he score goals in the First Division? I answered that query in my first season in the top flight and, had it not been for injury, I feel certain I would have equalled my goal tally in the 1985-86 season. Ah, but can he do it for England? The two goals against West Germany in my first full international proved nothing. I insisted before the game I could not be judged as an international player on just one game, whether I scored five or none at all. Nevertheless, it was a satisfying way in which to begin. The challenge remains. But then Kerry Dixon has always responded to a challenge as Brendan McNally, Maurice Evans and John Neal will surely testify.

The challenges promise to be even greater in the years ahead. I am still relatively young and yet the professional life of a footballer is so short-lived. Already, I have begun to lay plans to secure my future once the days of prolific goalscoring have come to an inevitable conclusion. Two close pals of mine John Dolan and Denis Diggin have got me interested in the building trade. I have worked with both of them on and off during the past couple of years and our association has provided me with a invaluable insight into their trade which appeals to me. I've recently acquired a property in Reading, the town where it all began for me as a professional footballer. Here I intend to set up a hairdressing business which might suit my sister Jane.

But my passion for football is enduring. The prospect of becoming a manager or player-coach appeals greatly. Yet, as I approach the 1986-87 season I am still only twenty-five and I intend to score many more goals and enjoy a lot more winning. I believe that a goalscorer should be at his peak between the ages of twenty-eight and thirty and by the time the next World Cup comes around I'll be slap bang in the middle at twenty-nine. But an unhappy Kerry Dixon would mean an unsuccessful Kerry Dixon. That's why the two hour meeting which took place before the 1986-87 campaign, between myself and the manager John Hollins, plus coach Ernie Walley was absolutely vital.

A suitable period of time had elapsed since the bitter disappointment of being left out of the final game of the previous season but the hurt and embarrassment of discovering my omission in the newspaper columns had not been eroded. I did not approach the meeting with hackles raised and blood boiling. I had been able to give a great deal of time, thought and consideration to the unsatisfactory situation which had prevailed in the latter months of the 1985-86 season. I knew that several top clubs would be interested in signing me should Chelsea consider me to be surplus to their requirements but I had no burning desire to leave Stamford Bridge. The club had been good to me since my signing from Reading and my relationship with the supporters, who I rate as absolutely first class, was fantastic.

The manager began by insisting my future was at Chelsea and that there was no way he wanted me to leave the club. He defended his decision to leave me out of the team for the final match of the previous season at Watford, explaining that it would have been foolish of me to risk injury before the World Cup. Mr Hollins made it clear that he believed Chelsea's opportunity to win the League Championship in the 1985-86 season had diminished drastically because of my stomach injury and the untimely suspensions of David Speedie. He was determined to avoid this situation in the future and that was why he had gone out and spent £400,000 on Gordon Durie. Now Chelsea would be able to enjoy the luxury of four first-class strikers available for selection. The manager went on to say that I remained a highly-valued member of his plans and his team for an even more determined attempt at winning the League Championship in the 1986-87 season. Our conversation succeeded in soothing the hurt and uncertainty I had experienced at the end of last season. I was immediately much more contented in my own mind and I can only hope that situation will prevail for a long time into the future. Now is the time for action and not words. In the meantime, I intend to dedicate myself to winning all of the game's major prizes. My burning ambition is to appear in a FA Cup Final at Wembley. I am determined to make the most of every single day I am fortunate enough to be a professional footballer. Deep down inside I know the best is yet to come for Kerry Dixon.

INDEX